WHAT IS VITAL IN RELIGION

WHAT IS VITAL IN RELIGION

Sermons on

Contemporary Christian

Problems

by

HARRY EMERSON

FOSDICK

HARPER & H|B BROTHERS

New York

Library of Congress catalog card number: 55-8522

Acknowledgments   The author wishes to express his appreciation to the following publishers and agents for permission to quote from their copyrighted works:

Mrs. George Bambridge, Doubleday & Company, Inc., the Macmillan Company of Canada, Ltd., and A. P. Watt & Son, for "If" and "Sussex" from *The Five Nations* by Rudyard Kipling.

Brandt & Brandt for "Dirge without Music" from *The Buck in the Snow and Other Poems* by Edna St. Vincent Millay.

Burnes, Oates & Washbourne for the selection from *Hound of Heaven* by Francis Thompson.

Harper & Brothers for "Indifference" from *The Unutterable Beauty* by G. A. Studdert-Kennedy.

The Macmillan Company for "Tomorrow" by John Masefield.

Contents

Preface

Paul, in the second chapter of his letter to the Romans, argues with his fellow Jews about what matters most in the sight of God, and in the course of his argument, as Dr. Moffatt translates it, he uses an arresting phrase: "a sense of what is vital in religion." The achievement of *that* is profoundly needed in our contemporary Christianity.

The divisions which produce our Protestant sectarianism are caused for the most part by concerns that are not vital. They are secondary, peripheral, irrelevant to the central meanings of the Christian faith. We never will get together until we see with deepened insight what is really vital in religion.

Moreover, the obstacles which keep many hungry and inquiring souls out of our churches are commonly these same extraneous, unessential matters. Today the need is deep for the indispensable vitalities of Christian faith; and to see them clearly, present them persuasively and live them devotedly is the importunate task of our churches.

I use Paul's phrase as the title of this book of sermons, not because these discourses deserve the apostle's designation, but because they do represent the ideal at which the discourses aim.

I have included a lecture on "Faith and Immortality," which is quite as much a sermon as it is a lecture. It summarizes my convictions about life after death and, because of that, I have let it stand as I delivered it at the Union Theological Seminary in New York, although two or three illustrations and quotations and a few sentences are repeated from sermons published many years ago.

This is my last volume of sermons, and with it goes my inexpressible gratitude to the many friends whose encouragement has sustained my ministry for over half a century.

HARRY EMERSON FOSDICK

Boothbay Harbor, Maine
July 15, 1955

WHAT IS VITAL IN RELIGION

Finding God in Unlikely Places

As we think about finding God in unlikely places we may well begin with the familiar hymn, "Nearer, my God, to Thee." Despite its popularity, many of us do not live up to it.

> Though like the wanderer,
> The sun gone down,
> Darkness be over me
> My rest a stone—

that is not a likely place to feel nearer to God.

> So by my woes to be
> Nearer, my God, to Thee—

that is not easy. We naturally find God in life's lovely experiences. "Praise God from whom all blessings flow"—that is where we find him, in our blessings. But when darkness and disaster come we commonly cry, Where is God?

One Englishman recently said this: "I don't know what I believe, but I don't believe all this God is love stuff. I have been in two world wars. I have been unemployed eighteen months on end. I have seen the Missus die of cancer. Now I am waiting for the atom bombs to fall. All that stuff about Jesus is no help." Well, did you never feel like that?

This morning we study the kind of person who, in such difficult situations, does not lose God, but finds him. We will be back in New York in a moment, but we start far from here, out in the wilderness of Sinai some thirty-two centuries ago, where Moses, facing a desperate situation, heard the divine voice say: "The place whereon thou standest is holy ground." Into that wilderness Moses had fled, a refugee from Egypt. In anger he had killed an Egyptian taskmaster who was beating an Israelite and, compelled to flee, had escaped into the desert to lose himself in the Bad Lands. Whether one thinks of the public evils of his time under Pharaoh's tyranny, or of the slavery of his people in Egypt, or of his own personal fall from being the son of Pharaoh's daughter to facing the niggardly life of the sheep range, he was in an unpromising place, and it was news to him when amid the sagebrush and the sand, the arresting message came that *that* was holy ground.

Far from being merely thirty-two centuries old, that scene is here in this congregation now. We find God in life's lovely things. Yes! God is in life's lovely things, but sooner or later all of us come to the place where, if we are to find God at all, we must find him in a wilderness. How we admire people who do that! When Helen Keller says about her blindness and deafness, "I thank God for my handicaps for through them I have found myself, my work and my God," that is something! I can find the divine in the Ninth Symphony or in sunsets when the sun, supine, lies "rocking on the ocean like a god," but to find God where Helen Keller found him, or Moses, that calls for insight.

Today we all need that insight. Not only does life land each of us in an unpromising situation, but our whole era is tragic, desperately tragic. How does one find God here? Yet some of the most momentous discoveries of God in history have been made in just such situations. A verse in the Book of Exodus has fascinated me for years, but I never have dared to preach on it.

Here it is: "And Moses drew near unto the thick darkness where God was." What a place to find God! Nevertheless, that kind of experience has made history.

In 1754 George Washington in his early twenties was on a tough spot. He had been defeated at Fort Necessity. He was accused of taking hasty action before reinforcements came so as to get all the glory for himself. His officers were called "drunken debauchees." His report on French plans was denounced as a crooked scheme to advance the interests of a private land company. It looked like the end of George Washington. But now Douglas Freeman, his biographer, looking back writes this: "Just when one is about to exclaim about some mistreatment, 'What an outrage!' one reflects and says instead, 'What a preparation!'" So from Moses to Washington holy ground has been found in a wilderness. What a preparation!

What went on inside Moses that made possible his discovery of holy ground in the wilderness? First, he found something to be angry at. He had been brought up as the son of Pharaoh's daughter, living a soft life, a playboy, it may be, at the royal court, but as maturity came on he began to be angry. How he must have fought against it, this disturbing indignation against something intolerably wrong, the slavery of his people! The more he grew up, however, the angrier it made him, until one day, seeing a Hebrew slave beaten by an Egyptian taskmaster, he was so incensed that he slew the taskmaster.

That was foolish. That did no good, but at least this is to be said for Moses, he was no longer a playboy. He was angry at something unbearably wrong. That was the beginning of the real Moses. His anger needed harnessing but it was basic to all that followed.

Said Martin Luther centuries afterwards, "When I am angry I preach well and pray better." Said William Ellery Channing, the great New England Unitarian minister, "Ordinarily I weigh one hundred and twenty pounds, but when I am mad I weigh a ton." Anger is not ordinarily presented as a Christian virtue, but remember our Lord, of whom our earliest gospel says that when he saw a deed of mercy being held up by a ceremonial triviality, he "looked round about on them with anger"; and when he saw little children being roughly brushed aside, he was "moved with indignation." Paul did write the thirteenth chapter of First Corinthians on love, but he also said, "Be ye angry and sin not." That is to say, control it, harness it for good, but still in the face of some evil you are not a Christian if you are not angry. Great character is not soft; at its very core is indignation at some things intolerably wrong.

So in his grim generation Moses began his discovery of holy ground, and when he came down from Sinai he carried with him ethical convictions that have shaken the centuries: "Thou shalt not kill." "Thou shalt not commit adultery." "Thou shalt not steal." "Thou shalt not bear false witness against thy neighbor." "Thou shalt not covet." His indignation against evil got him somewhere.

Need I expand the application of this to ourselves? Look at our world! It is hard to find God here, we say. Well, we can start. We can see the evil here that ought to arouse our indignation. We can see the everlasting right here calling for our backing and support. We can at least quit our moral apathy and wake up to the momentous issues of right and wrong in our community, our city, our nation. That is where Moses started when he found holy ground in the wilderness.

This start, however, led him to a second stage: Moses in the wilderness confronted Moses. He had never had such a searching look at himself before. Outward wrongs were there demanding that someone set them right but, if Moses was to help, he had to tackle Moses. We had better get this austere aspect of our theme into the picture, because the whole idea of seeing divine meanings in life is so commonly sentimentalized.

> The poem hangs on the berry bush,
> When comes the poet's eye;
> The street begins to masquerade
> When Shakespeare passes by.

That is true. Life is just as rich as we have the capacity to see. But that lovely aspect of the truth is not the whole of it. To confront oneself in a wilderness, to be told that there is divine opportunity, is a soul-searching experience. Tackle yourself, God said to Moses.

Of course, Moses at first backed off from that. Who was he to do anything about the Egyptian situation? "Meek as Moses" is a cliché now. Moses was far from being meek in any soft sense but he was humble. All great character is humble. William Carey, one of the supreme figures in Christian history, a major pioneer in opening India to the gospel, in his elder reminiscent years said, "If God could use me, he can use anyone." Moses was like that, and when at last on Nebo's top he surveyed the Promised Land and recalled the long, long years in the wilderness, I can imagine him saying: "If God could use me, he can use anyone." So, of course, he shrank from God's formidable call at first, but not finally. He *confronted* himself until he *dedicated* himself. He found his vocation in the wilderness. That is the gist of it. By God's help, he would be Moses.

How often scenes like that have been the turning points in history! Once a man named Wilfred Grenfell landed in Labrador on a gala vacation cruise, visiting for fun a strange coast. Landing on that bleak, inhospitable shore, however, he wrote afterward, "I attended nine hundred persons who never would have seen a doctor if I had not been there." That got him! He had to come back. He had to identify himself with Labrador. A divine voice had said to him in a wilderness, "The place whereon thou standest is holy ground."

God is saying that to someone here today about some situation—personal, domestic, social, national. It is dreadful, we may be thinking. Yes, but if a situation is dreadful, then there is need. Tragedy is simply need spelled with different letters, and so opportunity to help is there. You can do something for somebody, not despite the fact that it is Labrador, but because it is Labrador. "The poem hangs on the berry bush, when comes the poet's eye." Yes, but the real miracle arrives when the poem does not hang on the berry bush, but is deep hidden in a wilderness, or in Labrador, or in some forbidding personal tragedy, and then comes the poet's eye. So the great souls have found holy ground in unlikely places; they have found their vocation there.

We come to grips with our central theme, however, when we follow Moses' experience to a deeper level. In this encounter with right against wrong, in this self-dedication for his people's sake, he came face to face with God. Whatever may have been his idea of God, it is clear from the record that he had not in the least expected to meet his God there. What kind of situation was that in which to encounter God?

Many of us are precisely in that state of mind. We habitually talk of God in terms of love, beauty, goodness so that when we face a situation in our personal experience or in the world at large where love, beauty, goodness are singularly absent we lose all sense of God. Where is he? we ask. Our modern liberalism has contributed to this state of mind. Sings James Russell Lowell,

> God is in all that liberates and lifts,
> In all that humbles, sweetens and consoles.

That is true. Wordsworth sings of God as

> A presence . . .
> Whose dwelling is the light of setting suns,
> And the round ocean and the living air,
> And the blue sky, and in the mind of man.

That is true. But if the *only* God a man has is a God who thus is seen in the lovely things of life—its beauty and graciousness, the light of its setting sun, its liberating and consoling hours, then when he finds himself in some tough, dismaying experience in a desert where beauty, goodness and loveliness are absent, where has his God gone? In days like these I need the God who encountered Moses in the wilderness; who challenged Grenfell in Labrador, the God who confronts man in unlikely places.

As a matter of historic fact, some of the most memorable encounters with God in history have been of that type. Moses in the desert; the great Isaiah in Babylon with his exiled people; Job, out of his tragic calamity saying, "I have heard of Thee by the hearing of the ear, but now mine eye seeth Thee"—the Old Testament is full of such experiences. As for the New Testament, there is Calvary. My soul! Crucifixion is not lovely. Who, casually looking on, would have thought God there? But countless millions since, with hushed and grateful hearts, have seen that Calvary was holy ground. It is no accident, I tell you,

not physically in Babylon

that man thus finds in tragic situations some of his profoundest insights into the divine. Soft occasions do not bring out the deepest in a man—never! Rather in formidable hours when loyalty to the right means the risk of everything, perhaps life itself; in dismaying generations when right is on the scaffold and wrong is on the throne; in personal calamities when God is no mere frosting on life's cake but the soul's desperate necessity, then have come man's profoundest religious insights and assurances. Where did Jesus say, "Not my will but Thine be done"? In Gethsemane. When did Luther write, "A mighty fortress is our God"? When he was risking his life. When did Sir Thomas More say, "I die, the king's good servant, but God's first"? On the scaffold.

I do not know where this truth hits you but for myself, now in my elder years, I bear my witness. My deepest faith in God springs not so much from my Galilees, where God clothed the lilies so that "Solomon in all his glory was not arrayed like one of these," but from times when the rain descended and the floods came and the winds blew and beat, and God was there so that the house fell not. You know the familiar argument that the world is such a mess, its evil so senseless and brutal, that we cannot believe in God. Well, the world's evil is a great mystery. It raises questions which none of us can answer, but over against the souls who because of the wilderness surrender faith in God I give you today the souls who found him in the wilderness. They are a great company. Let us look at some of them.

Can you think of anything much worse than being a hopeless alcoholic? That's a wilderness for you. Well, here is my friend, Mrs. Marty Mann. She was there. Fifteen years ago she was in that hell. Listen to her story of what happened then. "In the depths of my suffering," she writes, "I came to believe, to believe that there was a power greater than myself that could help me, to believe that because of that power, God, there was hope and help for me." So in the wilderness she found God, and like Moses she is today leading many from the desert to the promised land.

Or, can you think of any much tougher situation a nation could go through then Britain experienced in the last war? I quoted one Englishman who lost God then, but Edward R. Murrow tells us, "In the autumn of 1940 when Britain stood alone, when the bombers came at dusk each evening and went away at dawn, I observed a sign on a church just off the East India Dock Road; it was crudely lettered and it read, 'If your knees knock, kneel on them.'" Thank heaven! the power to find holy ground in a wilderness did not die out in England and with it came, what Edward Murrow calls, "steadiness, confidence, determination."

Or, let me be autobiographical, as I trust some of you are being now. In my young manhood I had a critical nervous breakdown. It was the most terrifying wilderness I ever traveled through. I dreadfully wanted to commit suicide but instead I made some of the most vital discoveries of my life. My little book, *The Meaning of Prayer*, would never have been written without that breakdown. I found God in a desert. Why is it that some of life's most revealing insights come to us not from life's loveliness but from life's difficulties. As a small boy said, "Why are all the vitamins in spinach and not in ice cream, where they ought to be?" I don't know. You will have to ask God that, but vitamins *are* in spinach and God is in every wilderness.

Out of my stony griefs
Bethel I'll raise;
So by my woes to be
Nearer, my God, to thee.

Indeed consider not only personal situations but our world situation now. Think of the calamitous era of the American Revolution, so terrific that many then could perceive nothing but chaos and tragedy. Yet beneath the surface see what was going on. The thirteen colonies had been for years at bitter odds, sometimes at swords' points with one another. Then in 1774 at the first Colonial Congress, Patrick Henry made a speech in which he said this, "Throughout the continent government is dissolved. Landmarks are dissolved. Where are now your boundaries? The distinctions between Virginians, Pennsylvanians, New Yorkers, New Englanders are no more. I am not a Virginian, I am an American." See what was going on for those with eyes to perceive! A nation was being born. One of our contemporary historians describing that scene exclaims, "Forty-three delegates sat spellbound, hypnotized altogether. It was crazy what they had just heard; they knew it was crazy; an *American*, in God's name what was that?" But Patrick Henry was right and he would be right again if he could be here with us and beneath all our seething turmoil could see the emergence of new germinative ideas of world unity and world citizenship. This era too is holy ground. Play your part in it, large or small, against the little-mindedness, the prejudices, the hatreds that divide individuals and neighbors, races and nations. When Rip van Winkle went to sleep the sign over his favorite inn was George III; when he woke up the sign was George Washington. He had slept through a momentous revolution. Don't do that now! This is holy ground and God is here.

Now a brief final word. When any man thus finds God in unlikely places one may be fairly sure that he first found God in some likely places. Some beauty touched his life, some love blessed him, some goodness made him aware of God. If you have that chance now to discover the divine don't miss it! It's not easy to find God in unlikely places. Start now by finding him in a likely place. Beauty, goodness, loveliness are here, nobility of character, unselfish sacrifice, moral courage, and lives through which a divine light shines like the sun through eastern windows, and Christ is here too, full of grace and truth, in whom we see the light of the knowledge of the glory of God. Find God in these likely places that you may find him in the unlikely places too.

Having a Faith That
Really Works

IN a depressed mood Carlyle said once, "God sits in heaven and does nothing." We might shrink from such brusque expression, but many of us have a religion of which that is pretty much the truth. We intellectually believe in God—theism rather than atheism seems the more probable hypothesis—but we should be immensely surprised if we caught God doing anything. Over against that kind of religious faith we put today a verse from the 118th Psalm:

> This is the Lord's doing;
> It is marvelous in our eyes.

The writer of that Psalm had doubtless always believed in God. Now, however, something had happened. We do not know in detail what that saving experience was whereby, as he said, the Lord had set him "in a large place," but it changed the whole complexion of his life, and made a new thing of his religion. This God he had believed in had now done something. His religious faith had actually worked. God, who may have seemed to him to sit in heaven and do nothing, had, as it were, come to life and acted, so that no longer was the Divine a mere object of belief, but an experienced factor in daily living, available power to be counted on, operative in the world of events. Of definite experiences he could say, "The Lord's doing; . . . marvelous in our eyes."

The vital sense of reality in that kind of religious faith cannot be mistaken, and it presents a striking contrast with much of our common Christianity. Many of us believe in Christian ideas which we have inherited or argued ourselves into accepting. We believe in Christ. We agree that the Christian church is a useful, necessary institution, and should be supported. We consent in general to the Christian ethic, and think the world would be better off if it were more lived up to. So, we are Christians. That is, we are not Buddhists, nor Hindus, nor Muslims—no, nor atheists, nor even agnostics. But something is missing, my friends, something that makes the difference between formal, conventional religion, and its vital transforming reality. That something the Psalmist discovered, and we need to discover it too.

What an exciting experience it is when something we have merely believed in suddenly works! The scientists in their laboratories know what that experience means. Here is an idea that seems true—the arguments for it are good, the probabilities promising. This combination of chemical elements ought, so it would seem, to produce the desired result; this remedy, let us say, might cure this disease. So the scientists build hypotheses, argue theories, set up controlled experiments, until the day comes, worth all the labor it may cost, when, my word! the idea works. It is not merely an idea any more, but a force now, a power released into the world, that can do things. That is one of the most exciting of man's experiences. The modern scientist does not, I presume, like Archimedes, leap naked from his bath and run about the streets of the city crying, "Eureka!" but he must feel like it.

This Psalm reflects that experience in the realm of religion. Exultant astonishment is unmistakable here. Belief in God has turned into surprised discovery: God actually does things; he is not just a theory; he is energy, power, a doer of deeds.

The records of vital religion are full of the Psalmist's experience.

This man, for example, faced an impossible situation. His troubles were more than anyone could be expected to endure. They towered up over him until fear, that Svengali of the soul, began hypnotizing him, saying: You cannot take it; you are going to crack up. Indeed, he thought he would crack up until, remembering some things he had heard, he turned within and, as a last desperate resource, went far down where the deep sources of the spirit touch the nether wells, and lo! something happened. As really as in a scientific laboratory an experiment works, this worked. When far within himself he sought power, he touched not nothing but Something. So he did not crack up. He turned that most difficult crisis into a spiritual victory, and neither he nor his religion has ever been the same since. Were you to talk with him about it he would say: Man, this Christian religion actually works!

Or this man could not get himself together. He was not one self but many. Like Lincoln, in Robert Sherwood's play, he could say of himself, "You talk about civil war—there seems to be one going on inside me all the time. . . . One of these days, I'll just split asunder, and part company with myself—and it'll be good riddance from both points of view." On this unhappy, dissevered self our friend's volition labored in vain. The more he tinkered with himself, the more distracted he became. Then something happened. A Power greater than himself laid hold on him, and lo! committing himself to that Power greater than himself, he ran into an astonishing consequence: he was pulled together! He became integrated, coherent, one-directional! And if you ask him about it, he will say: Man, that was the Lord's doing, and it is marvelous in my eyes!

Or here is another man who, wronged by his enemies, accumulated resentment until ire and anger dominated him. Such hatred did no harm to his foes, but it made him a sick, embittered soul. We say that physical germs cause disease, but here is a sentence from one of the latest books on the subject: "A strong resentment is just as likely to cause disease as is a germ." So this man was literally sick with his embitterment. Then something happened. He read the "Sermon on the Mount," and decided to try an experiment. He began praying for his personal enemies, as Jesus did. It went hard at first, but by and by he succeeded. Negative attitudes of anger and malice gave way before constructive goodwill that could even forgive if the chance came, and in secret prayer could wish well to his foes. If you think that made him soft, you do not know the man. Was Jesus soft? But it did make him a healthy soul again, as if a clear northwest wind had blown the fog away. And if you ask him about it, he will say, with an accent of astonishment still lingering: Man, this Christian religion does actually work!

The list is endless of these saving experiences to which the Psalmist's words apply, and surely it is a pity that with this exciting, transforming reality of God's available power at hand, many of us have a religion of dull formality in which little happens, and our God sits in heaven and does nothing.

As we face this profoundly important matter, consider in the first place the intellectual absurdity of believing in God and not expecting marvelous results. To say on Sunday, "I believe in

God the Father Almighty," and then on Monday not look for extraordinary events to occur, does not make sense, for whatever else God is, he is spiritual power waiting to be released through our lives into the world. Of course marvelous things ought to happen.

Our prescientific forefathers took this aspect of religious faith in earnest by believing in miracles. They thought that anything might happen, saying of a thousand and one so-called miraculous occurrences, "This is the Lord's doing." We moderns have grown skeptical of such credulous belief. Stories of material miracles, coming to our minds, face an Ellis Island that peremptorily excludes them like enemy aliens. Indeed, even if we could believe things such as floating axheads, walking on the water, and such like, we would still ask, What does that prove anyway? Dr. Orchard was orthodox enough—he became a Roman Catholic —but he said once, "If I saw somebody walking on the water, I should not say, 'This man is divine.' I should say, 'Excuse me, do you mind doing that again because I didn't see how you did it?'" That is the modern attitude in a law-abiding universe, where we know that whatever happens must be the fulfillment of law, and not the breaking of it. So the whole realm of miracle, in the sense of broken law, has been excluded from modern thought.

I suspect that I am as modern-minded about that as anyone here, but I appeal to your reason. Does it make sense to throw away the old idea of miracle as broken law, and then substitute in its place the idea of God as tied hand and foot with his own laws, so that he can do nothing? That, in effect, is what has happened in the thinking of many moderns; that is why their God sits in heaven and does nothing; he cannot do anything;

his laws are in the way, they think, so that he cannot. To which, of course, the answer is obvious: Since when has knowledge of natural law limited personal action? Rather learn a new law in any realm, and we are set free to do a new thing. Get clearly in mind some new, unbreakable link of cause and consequence in chemistry, and lo! a whole new realm of possibility is opened up. Far from being imprisoning, the knowledge of law is one of the most liberating experiences man ever has. If we can heal diseases once incurable, conquer distance, build intricate machines, intelligently educate our children, and do many a needful thing once impossible, it is because we know the laws that underlie that realm. Learn a new law, and the law-abiding forces involved are put at our disposal. Well, God is not interned in the concentration camp of his own laws. Granted a real and living God, then all the law-abiding forces of the universe are at his disposal. So, the idea of miracle comes back again, not as broken law, but as law fulfilled.

God, for example, heals people who are sick, just as really as he did in the time of Jesus. Of course he does! Here is a recent utterance by one of our leading medical scientists: "It is not an overstatement to say that fully 50 per cent of the problems of the acute stages of an illness and 75 per cent of the difficulties of convalescence have their primary origin not in the body, but in the mind of the patient!" So! That from a medical man! Well, then, why should it be strange that the difference between health and illness, even life and death, sometimes lies in the question whether or not the patient has a tonic, undiscourageable faith, knowing what it means to be "strengthened with might by God's Spirit in the inner man"? Why should it be strange to see some come up from the very frontiers of death, saying,

> This is the Lord's doing;
> It is marvelous in our eyes.

This leads to a second matter of profound practical importance. We commonly make our religion an affair of belief, but merely to believe with the mind is hardly a start on the great experience of being a Christian. The real Christians have always made their faith a basis for day-by-day experimentation. It was something to try out, to venture on, to put to use, to get well by, to be transformed and empowered by, until, in one case after another, they came upon the exciting confirmation of their faith, saying, My soul! it does actually work!

This coming week, along with a considerable group of men representing well-known Christian enterprises in this nation, I shall attend a luncheon for a friend of ours, and we shall be congratulating him upon something God did in his life a generation ago. He was a total loss, then. His life was built on a wrong pattern, hardened in it by rigid habits that seemed unbreakable, and worse than going to waste. Then something happened. If you tried to tell him now that he did it himself, he would laugh at you. He could not do it himself. He did not even want to do it. No, he was transformed by the renewing of his mind. He surrendered himself to a Power greater than himself, and a miracle of spiritual law fulfilled and grace released took place, that believe-it-or-not Ripley might well put in his list. That was many years ago, and a distinguished career of Christian service as an influential layman bears witness to the fact that something really did happen.

From such experiences that stand out as indeed marvelous, through the whole range of our ordinary days, the Christian faith is meant not simply to be believed in, but experimented with. How few of us Christians do that! Give a scientist a new idea, and he at once thinks of it in terms of experimentation. Let us see what we can do with it! But give Christians the greatest idea that ever dawned upon the mind of man—God, our Father, spiritual reality behind and in our lives, available power for daily use—and how few of us translate that at once into experimental terms, saying, Come, let us see what this power can do with us and we with it.

One aspect of such experimentation lies in the realm of prayer. This is what prayer means—taking God in earnest, saying, If God is, let us keep in touch with him and see what he can do in, and for, and through us. Of course there are ignorant, incredible ideas of prayer. Anything can be spoiled by stupidity and superstition. The Bible itself says emphatically negative things about prayer. "When ye make many prayers, I will not hear"—the Old Testament says that; "Ye ask, and receive not, because ye ask amiss"—the New Testament says that. Prayer is not magic. A modern scientist like Dr. Alexis Carrel did not believe in magic, but listen to him: "Prayer is a force as real as terrestrial gravity. As a physician, I have seen men, after all other therapy had failed, lifted out of disease and melancholy by the serene effort of prayer." So,

> . . . More things are wrought by prayer
> Than this world dreams of,

in those who make God's power not simply an object of belief but a subject of experimentation, saying, Let us see what we can do with it, and it with us.

This leads our thought to a further matter. We just have said that to make God a mere object of theoretical assent, without doing anything with him, or letting him do something extraordinary with us, is only a caricature of religion. Now we ask why it is that this caricature is so prevalent among us. The answer is not difficult to see. Self-sufficiency is the reason. We feel adequate to handle our lives by ourselves. At least it does not occur to us that there is any other way of handling them. We may worship God on Sunday, but what do we need of him on Monday? So we believe in God on the surface of our minds, but in real life we do not practically count on anything except our own competence and skill. How common that way of living is, even in our churches! But that is the very essence of irreligion, even though we do say that we believe in God. Real Christianity is not just believing in God—"The devils also believe, and tremble," says the New Testament. Real Christianity is a daily personal, practical reliance on God.

Indeed, this religious way of living—becoming, that is, channels of a power greater than our own so that things beyond our competence are done through us—is so grounded in our essential nature, that it appears far outside the boundaries of so-called religion. Listen to Ralph Waldo Emerson, speaking about his authorship: "When I watch that flowing river, which, out of regions I see not, pours for a season its streams into me, I see that I am a pensioner; not a cause, but a surprised spectator of this ethereal water; that I desire and look up, and put myself in the attitude of reception, but from some alien energy the visions come." All excellent work is of that quality—inspired. It never explains itself by saying, I did it, but always by saying, It was done through me. A great soul never feels like a pool self-contained, but always like a river, a channel of more than individual grace and power.

> . . . every virtue we possess,
> And every victory won,
> And every thought of holiness
> Are his alone.

Moreover, this basic truth is evident not simply in personal life but in our world situation as a whole. Many today look at this scene of international tension and ill will and say, God sits in heaven and does nothing; but some of us see it otherwise. Gladstone said once, "The task of statesmanship is to discover where God Almighty is going during the next fifty years." Well, where God Almighty at least wants to go during these next fifty years is not altogether beyond our power to see, for with all the voices, not only idealistic but realistic, through which he speaks to us and brings his potent pressures to bear on us, he is saying to the world: Get together; you are fighting against the inevitable when you try to live in isolated alienation on the basis of your old political and imperialistic divisions; your agonies now are due to your stubborn resistance against a divine will stronger than your own, which ordains that there must be one human family, fighting against that, you will remain in hell; only when you surrender to that higher will can you find decency and peace.

God is not sitting in heaven and doing nothing. He is pulling us by the ideals of the prophets, and pushing us by realistic necessities, toward the goal he purposes, and it is we who are holding out against him. See! This spring day every tree hastens to make buds into leaves, and every blade of grass is tremulous with impatient life, but no tree and no blade of grass is the sufficient explanation of its own vitality. Something greater than them all is here; the spirit of life is abroad in the world, crowding itself everywhere on old dead forms, and making them bloom again. So is God present in this situation now, insistent on the death of old orders, and the birth of a new kind of world. And when at last that new world comes, as it will, some people, indeed, will say, We did it; but men and women of deep insight will be thinking of what God had to overcome in us before he got it done and, far from being self-complacent, will be saying, "The Lord's doing; . . . marvelous in our eyes."

It is of our own personal lives, however, that we may well think especially today, for this truth applies to all of us ordinary, commonplace people, in the midst of our daily tasks and hazards. Everyone knows Thomas Arnold, headmaster of Rugby. His illustrious career as a schoolmaster, his immense influence on English youth, his books—we know him. But who knows that he had a sister, a helpless invalid? "A daily martyr for twenty years," Thomas Arnold wrote, "during which she adhered to her early formed resolution of never talking about herself . . . enjoying everything lovely, graceful, beautiful, highminded, whether in God's works or man's . . . and in the end preserved through the valley of the shadow of death from all fear and impatience." Of her the world never heard, but who of us does not understand what Thomas Arnold meant when he wrote, "May God grant that I might come within one hundred degrees of her place in glory!" A personal victory like that is always more than one's own doing. What Ruskin said of the great artists is true of such radiant souls—their power is not "*in*" them, but *through* them"—and the results are marvelous in our eyes.

May some of us discover afresh that vital kind of religion! For this, my friends, is what keeps the Christian faith going, not alone creeds, rituals, organizations which by themselves would die and be forgotten, but this deep matter: millions of individuals, in bearing trouble, facing illness, overcoming resentment, escaping guilt, mastering sin, confronting death, discover that this Christian religion does actually work. "Wherefore we faint not; but though our outward man is decaying, yet our inward man is renewed day by day," and it is marvelous in our eyes.

The Great Christ and the
Little Churches

As Jesus in the Gospels confronts his contemporaries, one impression stands out—he is too big for them, much too big. That is the trouble they had with him; he would not stay inside their narrow limits. With their legalism, ritualism and religious conventionalities, how small they seem now, how local and provincial, while in him is something universal and eternal.

Nothing more challenging confronts us Christians today than the fact that this impression made by Christ of size, of universality of outlook and spirit, is distinctly not the impression made by our sectarian churches. I speak from inside the church, loving it, after a lifetime of ministry believing in it and loyal to it, but I am deeply concerned about its trivialities, its sectarian littleness. To have a Master and Lord who impresses even unbelievers with his universal range and sweep, and then to have churches, supposed to represent him, which impress even believers as much too petty and small-minded to meet the world's need—that is a tragedy.

In trying to get at this matter constructively, consider that there are inevitably two aspects to Christianity, as to any great religion—its universals and its local peculiarities. "Thou shalt love the Lord thy God with all thy heart, and with all thy soul, and with all thy mind, and with all thy strength, . . . and thy neighbor as thyself"—that is a universal. "Whatsoever ye would that men should do to you, do ye even so to them"—that applies to all mankind. "Be ye transformed by the renewing of your mind"; "Love is the fulfilling of the law"—no boundaries of race or nation hem such experiences in; they are universals. But, on the other hand, special modes of baptism, this or that way of serving communion, this or that idea of church government or of apostolic succession, many divergencies in creedal statement, and so on and on—these are local peculiarities that have arisen from our special cultural and racial history. Do not misunderstand me to be scornful about them. Local peculiarities have their place. Religion is like family life. Our homes have local peculiarities. Our houses belong to our special climate. Our individual methods of housekeeping, our cherished household traditions and celebrations, and all the small details that make a home our home, and not someone else's—such local traits in family life are not to be scorned. Yes, but in family life there are universals too. Without them nothing else matters. A man and a woman loving each other so much that they do not wish to love anyone else in the same way at all—that is a universal. All mankind knows of that experience. Far back in the Book of Genesis one runs upon it: "And Isaac brought [Rebekah] into his mother Sarah's tent, and took Rebekah, and she became his wife; and he loved her." Thus good families have both local peculiarities and universals, and so does good religion.

Indeed, Jesus himself had his local religious peculiarities. A loyal son of his people, he kept their feasts, attended their synagogues, loved their temple; and while he liberalized their ritual law, he observed it. But if you ask where his emphasis lay, it was on the universals. His God loving the whole world, his brethren all mankind, his ethical principles of universal application—

there was his emphasis, that made Christ Christ. It was a Jewish scholar, Dr. Klausner, who said that Jesus brought a conception of God and a morality applicable to all mankind, which broke down the barriers of nationality, and that because of this his people, Israel, clinging to the special peculiarities of their national religion, rejected him. What I am pleading for today, as about the most urgent matter facing present-day Christianity, is that, in this emphasis upon the great universals instead of the local peculiarities, our churches should follow their Master.

Let us guard ourselves now against one possible misunderstanding. When we thus stress the Christian universals, we are stressing the Christian profundities, not simply becoming broad but going deep. One danger in this sermon's emphasis is that in some people its consequence may be a kind of breadth that becomes shallowness. But Christ was not shallow—big, yes! so that the more one confronts him, the more one feels like Tintoretto when he tried to paint the sea. One day, throwing down his brushes in despair, he cried, "It keeps growing greater! Nobody can paint it." So Christ is great, but like the sea not in breadth alone—in depth too.

Some of you already have been saying to yourselves: This is a liberal preacher speaking, stressing the broad matters of the faith against the small and trivial. Very well, but I, who am a liberal, warn you about some so-called liberalism—superficial, shallow, breadth without depth. Beware of that! When we say that the truths of science are universal, are we not thinking of the profoundest truths of science, the great laws true everywhere and for all? So Christ, proclaiming the spirit's universal laws, started not so much by spreading out as by plunging deep. "When thou prayest, enter into thine inner chamber, and having shut thy door, pray to thy Father who is in secret"—that is an experience open to all men everywhere. Says a Hindu: "I make prayer mine inmost friend." Says a Muslim: "Allah is nearer to you than the great vein of your neck." That is a universal, but it is deep.

I am a liberal, impatient with the sectarian divisions of our churches, but the only way effectively to remedy this situation is not by becoming superficially broad, but by becoming profound. One God of all mankind—that's deep! One Spirit by whom we can be strengthened with power in the inner man— that's deep! One moral law, of which the Sermon on the Mount is our noblest utterance—that's deep! The dreadful fact of sin, and the desperate need of saviorhood—that's deep! "While we look not at the things which are seen, but at the things which are not seen: for the things which are seen are temporal; but the things which are not seen are eternal"—that's deep! And because it is so deep, it is universal.

Our Christian missionary enterprise, at its worst, forgets this fact and tries to transport our Western ecclesiastical localisms to the ends of the earth. The deplorable results of that have recently been stated frankly by the President of Nagpur College, India. "The day of denominational missions has in my opinion come to an end," he says. "It served its purpose . . . but it gave unintentionally not only the pure gospel of Jesus Christ but the Western structural organizational forms as well. In giving more than the gospel, its donation was not munificent but malignant. It sterilized the possibility of the genuine Christian community arising. . . . It sowed the seeds of division at its very inception, and all the travail that we now have to unite the churches is the result."

Not the localisms but the profundities of the gospel have wrought the real triumphs of Christian missions. One of our soldiers during the Second World War wrote home from a South Sea island: "Mother, these dear, black Fuzzy-Wuzzies saved my life, and they are teaching me to be a Christian." Nothing merely local so transformed those South Sea cannibals; the universals of the gospel did it. One of the greatest missionaries in India was C. F. Andrews. He once said to a friend of mine, concerning his approach to the Indian people: "I always assume that they are Christian; and after I have talked with them for awhile I sometimes see the light of Christ in their eyes." What a missionary!—sure that all men are made for the profundities of Christ's truth, and that Christ's truth is made for all men, so that if only he can rightly present the universals of the gospel, the old Psalm will come true again: "Deep calleth unto deep."

Consider now that when we thus stress the universal profundities of our faith, we are best meeting the arguments of many among us who are opposed to Christianity. You should read my mail and see the things that keep many people from being Christian. It is the local peculiarities they balk at. They have identified the gospel with them. A physician, it is said, hung out his sign in a community, and after waiting in vain for a practice put this addition on it, "Small fevers gratefully accepted." Our sectarian churches have too commonly welcomed small fevers, and many people, alas, have identified the Christian gospel with them.

What a privilege it is to deal with a man who so has thought of Christianity and, to his surprise, lead him back behind the local peculiarities until he has to confront the universal profundities! There at least his little arguments against Christianity do not apply. There at least he must acknowledge that he has been resisting not real Christianity, but its caricature. There at least he must face great matters that range far and go deep—the Sermon on the Mount, the parable of the prodigal son, the first chapter of John's Gospel, the thirteenth chapter of First Corinthians, the Letter to the Ephesians, "That ye, being rooted and grounded in love, may be strong to apprehend with all the saints what is the breadth and length and height and depth, and to know the love of Christ which passeth knowledge, that ye may be filled unto all the fulness of God." What universals!

In such terms, nothing small and sectarian about them, the New Testament, as a whole, presents Christ. So, there are many local kinds of food, but bread is not local; all mankind needs bread, and *that* the New Testament calls Jesus: "The bread of God," that "giveth life unto the world." Heaven help our churches now thus to stress the universals of our faith! Our shame is that in the gospel committed to us by our Lord, there is this breadth and length and height and depth, and we so have shifted our emphasis from that to our local peculiarities that we have become sectarian, partisan, provincial, cooped up in the confines of our isolated cultures. The gospel, in our hands, sometimes seems like a great ship, made to sail the seven seas, but so cluttered with small barnacles that it can hardly move. But of all eras in history this is a time for greatness in religion—greatness, not littleness! Thank God for the Christian leadership that today sees that, and for the inclusive ecumenical movements of thought and life in the churches which represent it!

To be sure, we shall continue to have our local religious peculiarities. We cannot live on universals alone. Let's not pretend to be bigger than we are! God may love the whole earth

equally, but we cannot. We all love some special places on the
earth, with their local settings. So Kipling sang:

> God gave all men all earth to love,
> But since our hearts are small,
> Ordained for each one spot should prove
> Beloved over all; . . .
> Each to his choice, and I rejoice
> The lot has fallen to me
> In a fair ground—in a fair ground—
> Yea, Sussex by the sea![1]

With a grateful heart each of us understands that, but to identify
Sussex with the whole earth, absorbed in Sussex to forget the
universal—that is a tragedy!

Look at the world today, desperately needing a profound
spiritual faith and life that will redeem and unite it! This is no
time for my special religious Sussex and yours to get into the
center of the picture. Our Sussexes are local. "The field is the
world," said Christ. "Ye are the light of the world." "God so
loved the world." Value your Sussex, but then remember, as
Kipling himself sang,

> What should they know of England who
> only England know?

So may the Church of Christ strike the universal note!

If here this morning there is, by chance, some individual who
has been identifying the great Christ with some small provincial-
isms, in God's name, face the real issue! What will you do about
the universal profundities of the Christian gospel?

[1] "Sussex" from *The Five Nations* by Rudyard Kipling. Copyright,
1903, by Rudyard Kipling. Reprinted by permission of Mrs. George Bambridge, Doubleday & Company, Inc., A. P. Watt & Son and The Macmillan Co. of Canada.

Our thought leads us further now to see that when the church thus stresses the Christian universals, it is making its distinctive and desperately needed contribution to the world. The world is certainly a sorry mess, and what helps make it a mess is not simply politics, nationalism, imperialism, and all the ungodly forces that divide us, but, alas, religion. Here is a major tragedy: religion which ought to unite mankind divides mankind instead, and helps to increase the world's confusion.

Dr. Hocking of Harvard has illustrated this by the analogy of language. Language should unite us, enabling us to talk together, understand one another and co-operate, but now mankind, plunged into one world before it is ready to handle one world well, faces not language but languages that separate us and make communication difficult. Thus, mankind, needing a great religion to unite it, faces instead religions that divide it. Well, some day we may get a universal language, and some day we may get a universal religion, but that is a long way off!

In the meantime, one momentous thing is going on in all the great religions. Facing this one world where isolation is no longer possible, the best thinkers in all religions see that their local peculiarities cannot persuade the world—never! As well try to persuade South Sea Islanders to live in Eskimo igloos, or Americans to live in bamboo houses. Thus local, thus peculiar to our special cultures, are the small sectarianisms of the various religions. Thoughtful Hindus, Buddhists and Muslims, therefore, are busy disentangling the universals of their faiths from the local peculiarities, preparing to confront the world, saying: This is essential Buddhism; this is essential Islam, the profound gist of the matter with the local accretions stripped off.

I am not saying that when this is done, the essentials of these various religions will agree. Of course they will not! There are profound differences. But I am saying that this endeavor to get at the universal essence of the great religions is one of the most momentous movements of thought in our time; that we Christians must meet it; that we cannot meet it with our petty sectarian divisions; that Christianity's hope now depends on presenting to the world the universal profundities of the gospel.

Would that we modern Christians were at least as big as some of the early church fathers, like St. Augustine! He lived in the fourth and fifth centuries. He knew competing pagan religions at their worst. He was a loyal Christian if ever there was one; he had ideas about theology and the church too rigid for most of us to accept; but at least he refused to confine Christianity inside any limits that would keep him from seeing its universality. Listen to him: "That which is called the Christian Religion existed among the Ancients, and never did not exist, from the beginning of the Human Race until Christ came in the flesh, at which time the true religion, which already existed, began to be called Christianity." So, he found Christianity in great affirmations that long before Christ men like Plato had made. When in spirits who had never heard of Jesus he saw Christian truth and life emerging, he saw the Universal Christ. If he had known that long before Christ Gautama Buddha had said, "Cleanse your heart of malice and cherish no hatred, not even against your enemies, but embrace all living beings with kindness," he would gratefully have recognized the Sermon on the Mount. He had his local religious peculiarities. Of course he did! But in his greatest hours he confronted the world with a universal Christ. So may God help us here in New York! God had better help us here, for in a city where all races, all nations, all religions meet, no mere localisms can ever win the day.

As for us, one by one, how easy it is to pick up from our

heritage and environment Christianity's sectarian customs and practices, to be after a fashion churchfolk, at least knowing our way around in the Christian conventionalities, but missing the deep experiences! How many such halfway Christians there are, at home in the local peculiarities but not in the saving profundities! Has someone here been content with that? Friend, it is not enough—not enough to live and die on—with the great experiences waiting. Ah, Lord, still too big for us, teach us the length and breadth and depth and height!

The Christ of History and the
Christ of Experience[1]

O NCE more on Christmas Sunday morning we come to the church to celebrate the Christ. But which Christ? Anyone, reading what is afoot in books and magazines today, can observe that two Christs are in the minds of men, often confused, often apparently contradictory: the Christ of history and the Christ of experience. "Now when Jesus was born in Bethlehem of Judaea in the days of Herod the king"—that is the Christ of history. "I live; yet not I, but Christ liveth in me"—that is the Christ of experience.

To some of us both these Christs are very real. One who has tarried long in Palestine thinks vividly of the Christ of history. To say, as a few have tried to say, that no such person ever existed, is to anybody who knows Palestine incredible. The story of the Gospels fits the land as a man's glove fits his fingers. Repeatedly the traveler says to himself: this is the country of the Gospels, this is the land of the record, across these hills the footsteps of the Master went. No scholar of any weight has ever doubted the historicity of Jesus.

Of course, there are many questions about whether he said this or that, did thus or so, about which Gospel in a given case is the more reliable, but such questions rise about any character

[1] A Christmas sermon.

34

who appears in history. To disentangle even the Lincoln of history from the Lincoln of tradition is difficult. So legends did grow up about Christ. That process is inevitable, and sometimes we think we can see what the legendary elements are and how they came to be. But this inevitable twining of the legendary around the trellis of a great character does not make us suppose that Lincoln, for example, did not exist.

So the Christ of history is real. From Nazareth to Golgotha we can trace the outlines of his life and see the major emphases of his teaching, but all this need not issue in vital Christianity. The Jesus of history lived long ago. His coming was the most significant event in the spiritual history of man and we do well to celebrate it in this radiant festival of the Christian year, saying: "Let us now go even unto Bethlehem, and see this thing that is come to pass." This alone, however, is not vital religion, and it does not become such until the Christ of history passes over into the Christ of experience. Because many do not achieve this transition they think of Jesus as an ancient figure, legendary and ideal, a kind of religious King Arthur, who centuries ago gathered his Knights of the Round Table and wrought chivalrous exploits. They even say about the historic Jesus:

> Dim tracts of time divide
>   Those golden days from me;
> Thy voice comes strange o'er years of change;
>   How can I follow Thee?

> Comes faint and far Thy voice
>   From vales of Galilee;
> Thy vision fades in ancient shades;
>   How should we follow Thee?

This problem of translating the Christ of history into the Christ of experience runs back as far as Paul. In a high, fine sense Paul was a mystic. That is to say, he could not be content with secondhand religion. Whatever religion he possessed had to be his own, intimately in him and part and parcel of him. Even Christ, therefore, could not suffice for Paul if by Christ you mean only a character in history. He said once, "Even though we have known Christ after the flesh, yet now we know him so no more," which is another way of saying, My Christ is more than just the Jesus of Nazareth who walked in Galilee. Once, when he was talking about the birth of Jesus, he said, "My little children, of whom I am again in travail until Christ be formed in you," which is to say, he felt the necessity, if religion was to be vital, of some such thing happening as centuries afterwards Phillips Brooks put into his hymn, "O holy Child of Bethlehem, . . . Be born in us today." And once Paul summed up this whole matter of translating the Christ of history into the Christ of experience by saying, "I live; yet not I, but Christ liveth in me."

On this Christmas Sunday morning, let us consider this serious matter:

> Though Christ a thousand times
> In Bethlehem be born,
> If He's not born in thee
> Thy soul is still forlorn.

To be sure, Christ did perform an objective, historic ministry and all of us, one way or another, share its benefits, even though nothing ever happens to us that could remotely be described as having Christ born in us. So Copernicus swung the gateway of a new era in astronomy, and though a man never heard of Copernicus he would share some of the benefits of his great work. If this were the birthday of Copernicus, you would feel a mild interest. He did his business long ago and fell on sleep and we are all indebted to him, and that is the end of it. But even if you were not a Christian you would feel that Jesus needs more intimate treatment. Were I to tell you of a family that always keeps Shakespeare's birthday, you would feel a subtler meaning there than the memory of Copernicus would evoke. The father of that family is a poet and when Shakespeare's natal day comes round they light the candles, call in a circle of congenial friends, and celebrate the evening with the master's poetry. You could not thus keep the birthday of Shakespeare without having the spirit of poetry within you. Even in that case the poet of history must somehow become the poet of experience.

Many Christians this week will not thus vitally keep Christmas. They will acknowledge that Jesus lifted the level of man's spiritual life and that they are immeasurably indebted to him, but vital Christianity has always had another note.

> But warm, sweet, tender, even yet
> A present help is he;
> And faith hath still its Olivet,
> And love its Galilee.

What does that mean? How can one reasonably and without sentimentality enter into that experience? What is the intelligible process which, without doing injustice to a man's mental faculties, causes the Jesus of history to become the Christ of experience?

In the first place, this transition occurs when we recognize the real nature of Jesus' greatness. There are two kinds of greatness. One is the genius of the gigantic individual. Napoleon Bonaparte was a prodigious character, and sometimes a man

studying him feels as he felt when first he saw the Grand Can-
yon of the Colorado—it is uncanny, weird, a stunt in nature as
though the earth had tried that sort of thing once but need never
try it again. When, however, you step into the presence of
another kind of man, like Michael Faraday, pioneering the
secrets of electricity, how different the impression is! Michael
Faraday is not primarily a gigantic individual. He is a revealer.
He uncovers something universal in the world that always has
been here and that men have not known. His greatness is not
so much in himself as in what he unveils, something woven into
the fabric of the universe from everlasting to everlasting, that
you and I can use and our children after us. Thus to reveal the
universal is the highest kind of greatness in any realm.

Between these two kinds of greatness, the uniqueness of the
gigantic individual and the glory of revealing the universal,
where would you put Jesus? Undoubtedly with the latter! He
kept insisting on it himself. "He that believeth on me, believeth
not on me, but on him that sent me." The glory of his life, as
he saw it, lay in the universal truth which he unveiled. "I am
the door," he said. You do not stop with the door; you go
through it to what it leads to. "I am the way." You do not end
with a way; you go along it to what it arrives at. So Jesus saw
his own significance in terms of the universal that he revealed,
and whenever anyone tried personally to flatter him he resented
it, and once he came back like thunder: "Why callest thou me
good? there is none good but one, that is, God." He was not
trying to be a gigantic individual; he was trying to reveal eternal
truth.

When, therefore, we endeavor to keep Christ back in history,
he will not stay there. He comes out of history. He leaves
Bethlehem behind him. He shakes the dust of Nazareth's streets

from his sandals. He comes to us in our modern life and says to us, I reveal the universal; the thing that I reveal is in you, flickering and dim, it may be, but in you; the life for which I stood belongs to all men and no man comes to his glory until he has achieved it. We cannot keep him back in history. What have geography and the calendar to do with universals? How much less can we keep Christ in Palestine or draw the boundaries of the first century around him. He is not simply the Jesus of history, but the Christ of experience.

This leads us to the second stage in the progress of our thought: if we think of Jesus as the revealer of the universal, we see at once that he is inescapable. Just as soon as Faraday had let loose in the world the meaning of electricity, man could not run away from it. We cannot let loose in the world a force like electricity and then avoid it. Henceforth electricity haunted men. It plucked them by the sleeve. It tapped them on the shoulder, saying, Use me! When once something like that has been unveiled it cannot be escaped.

So Christ let loose in this world a kind of life that mankind never has been able to escape. Make that just as definite and concrete as we will and see how true it is. "Whosoever would become great among you, shall be your minister; and whosoever would be first among you, shall be servant of all." Greatness measured by usefulness—he let that loose in the world. What a demented idea that seemed at first! Ask Pharaoh, ask Sennacherib and Xerxes! Ask even a philosopher like Aristotle! What a mad idea! Yet we never have been able to get away from it. No greatness except in usefulness—that haunts us. It has made the pomp of selfish emperors look ridiculous. It has stolen from the reputation of selfish wealth its glamor. "Benefactor of humanity" was the title men once gave their tyrants, but it became the title which Frenchmen gave to Pasteur, a paralytic and the son of a tanner, because of his usefulness. Emerson writes, "He is great who confers the most benefits." Poets catch the idea and sing,

> . . . that best portion of a good man's life,
> His little, nameless, unremembered, acts
> Of kindness and of love.

Even a Bismarck, hardened in power and pride, comes to the end of his days taking special satisfaction, among all the medals that hung upon his uniforms, in one conferred on him as a young man because he saved his groom from drowning. No greatness except in usefulness—you cannot escape that Christ.

Or "Blessed are the peacemakers"; "love one another; even as I have loved you"; "love your enemies, and do them good"—we cannot get away from that. Even Cicero, one of the noblest Romans of them all, so hated his enemy Clodius that, almost two years after the death of that enemy at Bovillae, Cicero was still counting time from that event: "the 620 day after the battle of Bovillae." But such unrelenting vindictiveness would seem contemptible even to common folk today. We cannot escape the haunting fact of Christ's goodwill.

Christmas Sunday is a fitting time to tell the story of General Pickett's baby. It was in the Civil War in those last slaughterous days when the two armies locked horns outside Richmond—the cruelest days of the conflict. Cold Harbor had been fought with terrific execution. Then, one night, the Confederate lines were lighted with bonfires and the Union sentinels, calling across the little space between the outposts, learned the explanation and sent word to General Grant's headquarters that the Confederates were celebrating General Pickett's newborn baby, word of whose arrival had just reached the army. By order of General Grant fires were lighted also in the Federal lines to help the Confederates celebrate the birth of Pickett's child, and the next day Union officers sent a graceful letter through the lines under a flag of truce, bearing to General Pickett the congratulation of his enemies. That story lights up a great truth. As you contemplate the scene you see that what was crazy there, mad, demented, execrable, was not the goodwill, the care for a family, the love of a child. That was sensible. But the hatred, the vindictiveness, the fratricidal strife—that was insane.

We cannot escape from that Christ who walks out of history to us today with his gospel of goodwill. He haunts even our legislative assemblies and in the councils of our governments is saying, "Blessed are the peacemakers."

Moreover, this inescapableness of Christ comes far down inside our individual lives. If he reveals the universal it is inside of us. Is there anybody here who has not tried to get away from that Christ within him? Is there anybody here who has not said, I will have no more of it; I will break its bands asunder; I will cast away its cords and have my own way? Have we ever entirely succeeded? There is something there we cannot be rid of. We have to deal with it one way or another, either to follow it, be true to it, or else be haunted by it. There is something in us that holds on and follows after and calls back.

In one of the greatest religious poems of the nineteenth century Francis Thompson calls it "The Hound of Heaven." Francis Thompson ought to know. He went to London as a student. He fell into evil ways. He lost his money. He became a drug addict. He went from bad to worse until he was holding horses' heads at the curbside for a sixpence. Few men ever were lower down than Francis Thompson. Yet, still, as he said, there came after him the pursuing feet of the Hound of Heaven:

> Still with unhurrying chase,
> And unperturbèd pace,
> Deliberate speed, majestic instancy,
> Came on the following Feet,
> And a Voice above their beat—
> "Naught shelters thee, who wilt not shelter Me." [2]

Can it be that there is no one here who is being pursued by that Hound of Heaven? We cannot keep Christ back in history. He presses on to become the Christ of experience.

This leads us to the next stage in the progress of our thought: that if all this is true, then Christ inevitably becomes the living realization of what we ought to be. He impersonates it; he incarnates it; he makes it picturesque and compelling. He is our realized ideal. This is worth saying because some of you may already have been thinking: Why call the ideal life "Christ"? Why not give it abstract names, like goodness, unselfishness, goodwill, magnanimity? Why give the abstract virtues a proper name out of history?

One answer to that can at once be given: ideas are poor things until they are incarnate. Did you ever fall in love with unselfishness? Of course not! Nobody ever falls in love with unselfishness any more than one falls in love with the Meridian of Greenwich. What we fall in love with is not unselfishness but unselfish people. It is when an idea becomes incarnate that it becomes powerful. Nobody understands human nature—I venture here to be dogmatic—until he sees that at the heart of us we are

---

[2] Used by permission of Burns, Oates & Washbourne, Ltd., and Mr. Wilfred Meynell, executor.

photographic plates taking pictures of people. We may think we argue ourselves into righteousness. We do not. Intellect and will are very important, but in this regard they are not primary; they are secondary. Primarily we are photographic plates taking pictures of people.

Somebody incarnates sin until it becomes irresistibly alluring —that does the business. Somebody incarnates goodness until it becomes fascinating and transforming—that works the consequence. Nothing ever vitally gets through to us until it is impersonated, and the photograph is taken on our souls. At the heart of us we are sensitive plates exposed to people.

Paul stated this truth in an unforgettable sentence. As Dr. Weymouth translates it: "All of us, as with unveiled faces we mirror the glory of the Lord, are transformed into the same likeness, from glory to glory." Just so! We face Christ until reflected in us he is reproduced in us. Paul uses the mirror figure because they did not have photographic plates in those days, but if they had I suspect he would have used that. We face Christ until his picture is taken on our souls. That is what had happened to Paul when he said, "I live; yet not I, but Christ liveth in me."

They call us modernists. Very well, let us be modernists! But remember that our modernism is not what modernism too often tends to become: a set of abstract hypotheses, a system of theoretical propositions. Our religion is impersonated. Christianity is Christ. And to know him and love him until his spirit is reproduced in us and the Christ of history becomes the Christ of experience—that is vital Christianity.

All this is incomplete, however, without the conclusion. There is really a Divine Presence which invades our lives. Sometimes Paul calls this Presence the Spirit—"Be filled with the Spirit."

Sometimes Paul calls it God—"filled with all the fullness of God." Sometimes Paul calls it Christ—"that Christ may dwell in your hearts through faith." Not of three experiences is he talking, however, but of one, the profoundest experience of vital religion, the indwelling, transforming presence of the Divine. To be sure, when a character in one of H. G. Wells' novels said, "I'm not a man but a mob," he spoke for all of us. We do have a miscellaneous, heterogeneous population in our souls, good, bad and indifferent, Dr. Jekyll and Mr. Hyde in all their various degrees, but always a Divine Presence is there too. We never completely escape him.

Paul also was a "mob." Read the seventh chapter of his Epistle to the Romans and see his inner turmoil, so contrary-minded that what he would he did not, and what he would not that he did. There was only one way out for Paul to unity and peace: to lift up into ascendant sovereignty the Christ within him, to identify himself with *that*, until that became his real self and all else was subjugated or sloughed off.

That is what the text means: "For me to live is Christ." I have heard that talked about as though it were theology. That is not primarily theology. That is primarily a bona fide psychological experience, a real transforming process that can go on inside a man, where he identifies himself with the Christ in himself until that is his real life and for him to live means Christ.

I never shall forget the day a lad came into my office, a whipped boy if ever there was one. He put his head down on his arms and would not so much as lift his eyes to look at me. And he might well be whipped. He was confessing a gross sin. Nor shall I forget how he did look at me when, after a half-hour's talk, I said, "You are a fine, clean, high-minded boy." "My God!" he said, "My God!" But I was right. He never would have come to me if there had not been that better side to him. It was that which was disturbing him. That was why he could not be a contented beast. His problem was somehow to identify himself with the Christ in himself till that became his real self and he sloughed off the rest.

You cannot keep Christ back in history. He is inside of every one of us and on this Christmas Sunday he is saying, Identify yourself with the Christ life, until the Christ of history becomes the Christ of experience. This is the central appeal of personal Christianity. I am weary of ecclesiasticism. I am often sick of controversial theology. But this is something deep and abiding.

Recall how Richard Wagner wrote some of his greatest operas. He played them on his own piano. He had no theater. He had no orchestra. He had no chorus. He had to play them on his own piano. He could not hear them as they would really sound orchestrated and rendered with many voices. He had to imagine how they would sound. So he wrote *Tristan and Isolde.* Years afterward he had not yet heard it. He could get no theater to produce it. He could listen to it only as he played it himself.

So it was with Christ. Long ago in Palestine he played the gospel on his own life. But you cannot adequately play the gospel even on his life; it takes an orchestra; it requires a chorus. It takes communities, cities, nations, the world. Jesus has never heard how his gospel would really sound. To enter into that problem, to catch his spirit, to reproduce his life in ourselves, our families, our nations, and our world until the Christ of history becomes the Christ of universal experience—that is Christianity.

Miracles of Character
Possible for All

SUPPOSE that you had been a disciple of Jesus in Galilee and long after he was gone you were setting down your recollections of him. What would you naturally remember first? Surely, one would recall the positive things that Jesus said and did, the creative acts that revealed the depths of his character and laid the foundations of his church. In the New Testament, then, watch one of his disciples, Simon Peter, now an elderly man, writing a letter to his fellow Christians in Asia Minor and in a glowing paragraph setting forth his recollections of the Master. Almost his first remembrance, as though like cream it rose to the surface of his memory, was not something that Jesus did but something that he did not do. "Who," writes Peter about Jesus, "who when he was reviled, reviled not again; when he suffered, threatened not." So! Peter was profoundly impressed by some things that Jesus did not do.

In that reaction, of course, Peter revealed quite as much about himself as about Jesus. The Gospels make plain that Peter was an ardent firebrand of a man, all tinder and temper, with vigor impetuously to act for good or ill. So with this temperament Peter confronted Jesus and what struck him was not alone what Jesus did but what Jesus did not do. Peter saw Jesus in positions where he, Peter, knew well enough what *he* would do—and Jesus did not. He was reviled and he reviled not again; he suffered but he did not answer it with resentment. He was caught in situations that would naturally call out bitterness, fear and dismay, but he was not bitter, frightened or discouraged. What was it in this strange man that underlay his incredible way of not doing the expected?

You have a friend, let us say, your affection for whom is deep and reverent. The chances are that your feeling for your friend does not depend simply on his creative deeds, acts that the world can see, however important they may be. You probably have sometime seen him stanch in a difficult situation. You would naturally have expected him to be embittered but he was not. He might have gone to pieces but he did not. It would not have been strange had he become cynical and disillusioned, but he was not. It is commonly the things that such people do *not* do that make on us the deep impression of quality and raise the question, What resource is in such folk to cause this inner miracle?

We cannot understand why Abraham Lincoln has such a hold upon our people without taking this into account. To be sure, he did things notable in history and yet it is not disparaging him to say that we have had greater statesmen than he. But there he is, deeper, I suspect, in the affection and reverence of the people than any other man. When almost everybody was bitter, he was not. When many voices called for vengeance, his did not. He was terribly hated, North as well as South. In one of the northern states I recall an outstanding citizen who concealed his first three names under initials, for they were "John Wilkes Booth." His father had named him in honor of Lincoln's assassin, so hated was Lincoln even in the extreme North. He was reviled but he reviled not again; he suffered but threatened not. "With malice toward none, with charity for all"! What some people have not done has made a tremendous impression on history.

This ought to be encouraging to us ordinary folk. Sometimes I am worried about the effect of preaching. We preachers so naturally hold up as ideals the supreme characters and careers, the great saints, apostles, martyrs, and Christ over all, that I should think men and women with routine tasks and ordinary opportunities, and the preacher too, when he takes off his pulpit gown and looks at himself in a mirror, might sometimes be more cast down than helped. How can we be Isaiah, Paul, Savonarola, Luther, Schweitzer, Kagawa, that preachers are always talking about, much less Christ? Well, to think what the great creative spirits *do* is one thing but to think of what we are considering today is another. Some very humble persons we have seen caught in positions where we might have expected them to be embittered and they were not, to be cynical and disillusioned and they were not, to be defeated and undone and they were not. They were only small shrines but a great miracle was wrought in them. One could almost say that Christ himself could not have handled *that* much better.

Such a life reminds one of the burning bush that Moses saw. It was not a great tree. It was only a bush. It was afire, says the old story. It should have burned up. On the basis of all natural expectation it should have been consumed, but it was not. Who of us, seeing a character like that, has not felt as Moses did—"And Moses said, I will turn aside now, and see this great sight, why the bush is not burnt"?

We are talking about this today because we are living in a generation when this miracle of character is critically needed. Consider, then, in the first place, that as we give our minds to it our thought is inevitably led to the dimension of depth in character. So much of our modern life calls for expansion of life but so little helps us with the dimension of depth! Science, for example, education, culture in general, and all the busy activities of the world demanding competence and ability expand life but they do not necessarily deepen character, and the dimension of depth is our crucial need.

In the life history of every sailboat there are days when you can spread your sails and be as expansive as you will, and go places. But there are also days when you have to reef your sails and look to your centerboard, and if, on days like that, when one might naturally expect you to capsize, you do not, the secret lies in a dimension which sails alone cannot supply. Mme. Curie, for example, was one of our generation's great personalities, an amazing synthesis of positive abilities, but if you read her life story carefully you will find that everything she ever did depended on something that she did not do. She was reared in Poland under circumstances so discouraging that on any ordinary basis you would have expected her to give up in her teens, but she did not. When she came to Paris, as it were on a shoestring, she lived in a garret and faced so many clossed doors that she might easily have been embittered, but she was not. When she and her husband were about to discover radium, all the laboratories in the university were denied her and she had to work in an old abandoned wooden shed that nobody else wanted, which might well have left her disillusioned and resentful, but it did not. At the climax of her wedded happiness, in the floodtide of her co-operation with her husband, he was killed one day by a truck on a Paris street, and she cried in despair, "It is the end of everything, everything, everything," and one might have thought she was finally going to pieces—but she did not.

As we consider the things she did not do that everywhere underlay and supported and made possible what she did do, one is confronting the dimension of depth in character—rootage, foundation.

This is one of the most revealing aspects even of a child. You may be gratified by many desirable things your youngster is doing but some day something may happen that, as with Peter remembering his Lord, if you live to be a hundred you will think of first. Sometime you may see your youngster in a tight place where his life, or perchance someone else's life, depends on him, where you might expect him to lose his head, but he does not; to be frightened, but he is not; to forget how to handle himself in his confusion, but he does anything but that. And when it is over, you will say to yourself: That youngster has stuff in him; he has character. It is amazing how impressive and indicative even in a child are the things he does not do.

We Americans naturally have Simon Peter's temperament. We are energetic, vigorous, impetuous. We are all for blowing on our hands and doing things to the world. But the times come, not personally alone but socially in a generation like this, when the world starts in to do things to us. Like a hurricane, terrific events tear through our generation's life. All around us are people who in a time like this might be expected to be cynical, and they are; might be expected to give up great faiths, and they do; might be expected to make up their minds that there is no God, and they become atheists. What is it that keeps a country from complete devastation when a hurricane blows through it? It is the trees that at a time when you might have expected them to blow over did not. What is it that keeps this world as decent and hopeful as it is? It is the men and women who in a time when you might expect them to be cynical, disillusioned, discouraged and out of faith, are not.

Let us take a further step and see how naturally our thought is led through the question of depth in character to the question of depth in faith. Of course, if by faith we mean credulity, all intelligent discussion stops. But faith is not credulity; faith is man's inner self-committal to convictions and causes and persons that seem to him supremely true and worth while. If that is faith's meaning, then obviously we cannot have depth of character without it. The real opposites of faith are cynicism, disillusionment, the sense of futility, the feeling that life came from nowhere, means nothing, and is going nowhither, and one need not argue at length that with these attitudes dominant, however charming and expansive a life may be, character lacks adequate underpinning and resource.

If someone says that this is a very difficult era in which to maintain great faiths in democracy, in the possibilities of peace, in Christ's principles applied to a world like this, in God over all, I agree. But in what other era was it ever easy? To which I can imagine some of my friends saying, The Victorian age. It would have been much easier then to hold great faiths. Very well, perhaps it would, but remember, it was in the Victorian age that John Stuart Mill cried out against "the disastrous feeling of not worth while." It was in the Victorian era when Rossetti despaired of international relations, and cried, "The earth falls asunder, being old." In the Victorian era Samuel Butler wrote his satiric and cynical novel, *The Way of All Flesh*. Remember that it was in the Victorian age that Matthew Arnold wrote,

> The sea of faith,
> Was once, too, at the full, and round earth's shore
> Lay like the folds of a bright girdle furl'd.
> But now I only hear

Its melancholy, long, withdrawing roar,
Retreating, to the breath
Of the night-wind, down the vast edges drear
And naked shingles of the world.

So, my friend, the chances are that if you are denying the great
faiths now you would have been denying them in the Victorian
age or any other. Depth of character grounded in depth of faith
never has been easy.

Do you think it was easy for Jesus? We so deify him, so lift
him out of the homely realism of his earthly life, that we lose
the vivid sense of the struggle he went through. He lived in a
terrific generation, worse than ours. Moreover, he reacted with
indignation and even scorn against the contemporary religion
of his time. I hear young people now blowing off steam against
religion and its representatives in church and theology, but they
cannot match Jesus at that. He raked the religious leaders of his
people fore and aft. His denunciation of current faith and practice bristles with indignation. The twenty-third chapter of
Matthew's Gospel is one of the most devastating arraignments
of religion and its leaders in all literature. And listening to him
so, one might have thought he was going to give up religion.
So! one would have said, he is through with religion! But he
was not. Deep beneath the forms of faith he laid hold on faith,
found the great religion that lies beneath religions—inner self-
committal to convictions and causes and persons supremely true
and worth while. Here, then, is Peter, long afterward remembering him and especially this strange differential quality, depth of
character grounded in depth of faith.

Most people are more or less alike—oh, by and large alike.
But once in a while one does run upon this differential quality.
It is as though we heard a voice out of a burning bush: "Put off

thy shoes from off thy feet, for the place whereon thou standest is holy ground."

Let us take now one more step and note how naturally our path leads through depth of character to depth of faith and then to depth of inner spiritual resource.

When George Matheson began growing blind and the girl he was engaged to turned him down because, naturally, she did not want to marry a blind man, he had every justification for feeling disenchanted and embittered, but, instead, he sang, so that we sing it yet, "O Love that wilt not let me go." We confront there depth of character, yes! depth of faith, yes! but something more —depth of interior spiritual resource. Matheson must have known something about prayer. So one of our American educators, frail in body but powerful in influence, said, "When I'm tired I just plug into the universe!" That is prayer. I hardly know a better practical description of it—plugging in on the universe. How do men live without that, or, at any rate, how do they get inner depth and stability so that when everybody is expecting them to be resentful, cynical and embittered, they are not?

Take this matter of magnanimity which so impressed Peter when he thought of Jesus. There is something moving to me in the spectacle of that old disciple looking back across the years to his Lord and first of all thinking of that—reviled, he reviled not again. Of course that particularly impressed Peter because to Peter's temperament that seemed incredible. On the basis of any natural human presupposition, such magnanimity is incredible. In the New Testament listen to what men did to Paul: "Five times received I forty stripes save one. Thrice was I beaten with rods, once was I stoned," and as one reads on and on one feels that there is ample justification for bitterness and resentment. Nobody could blame him for that. But read another passage from Paul: "Love suffereth long, and is kind; . . . is not provoked, taketh not account of evil; . . . beareth all things, believeth all things, hopeth all things, endureth all things. Love never faileth." There is something mysterious about that quality of life—depth of character, depth of faith, depth of interior resource.

The point of this sermon is that such character is open to us all. It is commonly seen in humble places. Genius often misses it but there are many ordinary folk in this congregation in whom it is beautifully exhibited. There are limits around what creatively we can do. But every one of us can leave behind a memory like this in the hearts of his friends: we saw him in a position where we expected him to be embittered and go all to pieces and he did not. This is no matter of piety alone that a man may talk about in church on Sunday and then forget. Even Rudyard Kipling in his popular poem, "If," in which he tries to sum up what he thinks makes up a man, is talking most of the time about this thing we are thinking of:

> If you can wait and not be tired by waiting,
>   Or being lied about, don't deal in lies,
> Or being hated don't give way to hating,
>   And yet don't look too good, nor talk too wise:
> .   .   .   .   .   .
> If you can fill the unforgiving minute
>   With sixty seconds' worth of distance run,
> Yours is the Earth and everything that's in it,
>   And—which is more—you'll be a Man, my son! [1]

[1] "If" from *The Five Nations* by Rudyard Kipling. Copyright, 1903, by Rudyard Kipling. Reprinted by permission of Mrs. George Bambridge, Doubleday & Company, Inc., A. P. Watt & Son and The Macmillan Co. of Canada.

A Religion That Really Gets Us

Sometime since in a personal consultation I faced a young woman about to go over to the Roman Catholic Church. Reared in a liberal Protestant home, with a good mind and an excellent education, the reasons she gave for turning to the Roman communion were important. She had always had a religion, she said, which belonged to her—her private possession. Now, however, she needed a religion that possessed her. She wanted a religion, she said, that talked to her intellect as geometry talks, not saying, It would be a lovely experience if you would only think this, but rather saying, This is the eternal truth whether you think it or not. She was hungry for dogma, for an authoritative voice with "something granitic in it," she said, that would confront her, proclaiming, This is the everlasting truth to which you must subject yourself.

At first sight many of us would not recognize ourselves in that young woman; we are not consciously hungry for dogma. And yet in our churches how many now are finding their religion inadequate for these turbulent days? They have had a religion of sorts, each one's faith according to his personal preference, as though to say, Everyone to his taste; some people like mushrooms and some don't; some thrive on this kind of faith and some on that—as you like it! So one college student set it down in plain English: "Most of us have a private religion of our own." But that youth would never say that he had a private science of his own. What if great religion also confronts us as great science does, saying, This is the everlasting truth; make it your private affair or not, this is eternally so about the universe? There would be strength in such religion for days like these.

For many of us the religious struggle of our youth was to get rid of dogma, break its intellectual bondage and achieve freedom. So we scrapped authoritative creeds, sometimes minimized doctrine, made belief a matter of as you like it, and called Christianity a practical way of life. Now, however, we find ourselves in a new generation with multitudes who never have had doctrine, whose problem is not at all to free themselves from dogma but rather to find somewhere some steady truth that they can honestly believe in and tie to. It is as though a whole generation had rebelled against some political tyranny and smashed it, but now, facing in consequence a chaotic society whose problem is not to escape from tyranny but from confusion, they cry out for government, some government that can bring order and claim allegiance.

We who live in theological circles, at any rate, are witnessing a strong tide of return to doctrine, to a fresh recognition that no religion can meet the deepest needs of these times if it cannot intellectually confront men with a proclamation of something that is really so, saying as Jesus did, "Ye shall know the truth, and the truth shall make you free."

This demand is rising now, for one thing, as a protest against the way some Christians have reduced Christianity to a practical, ethical way of life. To be sure it is that—an amazing way of life, the most worth while ever proposed, but today the Christian way of life faces a generation whose violence and moral decadence flatly contradict it. It is the Christian ethic that is in difficulty. During the last war an American lieutenant general made an address over the radio in which he said this: "Make yourselves into fighting devils now, not later. . . . We must hate with every fiber of our being. We must lust for battle; our object in life must be to kill; we must scheme and plan night and day to kill. . . . Since killing is the object of our efforts, the sooner we get in the killing mood, the better. . . . You are going to get killing mad eventually, why not now?"

Some liberals thought that they had simplified Christianity when they sidetracked its doctrine and made its ethic central, but now it is the ethic that is most denied. So we face the question: has the Christian ethic any standing ground in the everlasting truth about life? Are we really animals fulfilling our nature when we behave as we do, or are we children of God, sinning against our nature and against his eternal laws with our bloody violence, and so plunging ourselves into this earthly hell? Any answer we give to that towering question is doctrine.

For another thing, this demand for a religion that can proclaim something everlastingly so is forced on us today by the fact that the enemies of everything we care for most—our liberty, our democracy, our human dignity—are marching to the attack not with tanks and airplanes only but with doctrines. Nazism involved an ethic that is to us revolting, but it started with a philosophy; and, as for communism, no religious dogmatism is more strict and rigid than the doctrines of Marx and Lenin. Call these systems of thought ideologies if we will—what's in a name? We are facing today not simply a military or even an ethical conflict but an intellectual conflict, and at the heart of it the religious question rises: Is man only a thing, with no inherent rights and no eternal allegiance, or is man a child of God, with dignities, rights, freedoms, and an allegiance to the Divine that no man and no nation can annul?

While Hitler was rising to power the Roman Catholic Bishop of Berlin, Conrad Count von Preysing, publicly summed up in one article after another the whole Nazi doctrine, and then as Bishop of Berlin he called it a "terrible creed," and he ended by saying, "I must seriously warn you against such theories. . . . Change your mode of thinking! This is my appeal to you." So, the rebirth of Christian emphasis on doctrine is not first of all the Christians' doing; our enemies have forced it on us. Communism is not only a tyranny; it is a creed. It challenges not alone the church's ethic but the church's theology. If we are to meet that challenge we must proclaim the truth, as we see it, about what is everlastingly so. My friends, any religion that cannot do that today is a washout.

What kind of religion, then, have we as individuals with which to confront these days? Every one of us is bound to have a doctrine of some sort. We cannot live with anything without accumulating ideas about it; much less can we live decade after decade with the universe without having made upon our minds deep impressions from it that issue in beliefs about it. Granted that philosophy can be a very recondite and mystifying subject for experts only—as one bewildered man put it, like looking at midnight in a dark room for a black cat that isn't there. But today a man's philosophy of life takes on another aspect. Like it or not, we have to choose between the ideas that battle for supremacy upon the earth; and in that battle the Christian faith is a major competitor. Granted the nonsense that has been associated with the presentation of Christian doctrine, and even the justification of Dr. Will Durant's exclamation: "When will the

time arrive when men and women can attend church without
the need of checking their intelligence as they enter!" Yet even
that excuse will not avail us now. Our whole civilization confronts a conflict of doctrine, and the solemn words of Thomas
Huxley, the scientist, loom large today: "The longer I live, the
more obvious it is to me that the most sacred act of a man's life
is to say and to feel, 'I believe.'"

As we face this question, consider for one thing that the impression in some quarters that the central affirmations of Christian doctrine have been overthrown, is not true. The existence
of God, the fact of a moral order, the dependence of man on a
power greater than himself, the supreme revelation of the divine
character and purpose in Christ, the profound need of men to be
inwardly transformed by the renewing of their minds—such
affirmations of Christian faith have not been overthrown. Rather,
it is the alternatives to them that totter and fall under the shock
of this present crisis.

Only a few years ago the chief alternative to Christian doctrine among high-minded people was nontheistic humanism, a
creed which said that the existence of God did not matter, that
man himself was the sufficient object of our faith—man, his goodness and his ability, by himself, to make a glorious world. Well,
look at man by himself and repeat if you can that creed today,
that his goodness is the sufficient object of our trust!

Moreover, back of that doctrine of nontheistic humanism
lurked the doctrine of materialism, that there is nothing creative
in this universe except protons and electrons going it blind. I
cannot believe it. If there is not a living God of moral judgment
in this universe, I can make no sense of what I see. As another
said about the law of gravitation, when a man walks out of a

ten-story window and takes the consequences, he is not breaking the law of gravitation—he is illustrating it. So this disastrous generation illustrates the fact of a moral order here.

The ancient Greeks had two words that summed the matter up: *Hubris* and *Nemesis*. *Hubris*—a word untranslatable in English—stood for everything we mean by pride and arrogance, by overbearing insolence and the cruel use of power, and the Greeks said the gods hated that above all else, and that whenever *Hubris* appeared, *Nemesis* followed—the judgment of Zeus on all that puffs itself up with arrogant presumption. Well, in Hitler's case and Mussolini's we have seen that illustrated, and I for one feel sure that the Kremlin will follow in their steps. As the Psalmist put it,

> He hath made a pit, and digged it,
> And is fallen into the ditch which he made.

When Lorenzo de Medici, dictator of Florence, lay dying, he sent for Savonarola to hear his confession and absolve him. "Sire," said Savonarola, standing at the bedside of the dying tyrant, "God is good, God is merciful; but for his forgiveness three things on your part are necessary." "What are they?" whispered Lorenzo. "First," said Savonarola, "you must have a sure and lively faith in the mercy of God." "I have that," said Lorenzo. "Then," said Savonarola, "you must restore all your ill-gotten wealth, or at least charge your sons to restore it in your name." Lorenzo hesitated and then nodded assent. Then Savonarola towered up like an avenging angel and said, "Finally, you must restore the liberties of Florence." And they say that Lorenzo, his eyes flashing anger, turned his face to the wall in refusal, as though to say, Sooner hell than that! Now, however, in the retrospect of history it is Savonarola who still holds the field, representing something in this universe more powerful than any Lorenzo, the *Nemesis* that inexorably follows on the heels of *Hubris*. My friends, if there is nothing in this universe but protons and electrons going it blind, why should *Hubris* bring *Nemesis*? No, not the great affirmations of religious faith but their alternatives are shaken and tottering today.

To a preacher it is interesting to see this conviction expressed with clarity and power not by theologians alone but by laymen. This sermon was well on its way when I ran upon an article in *Fortune*. Here is a layman talking to us. He wants us to get back to what he calls "the absolutely stupendous interpretation of life and history that Christianity offers." See, he says, as he writes about this last generation, "the people in general . . . did not believe that the truth would set them free, but they were sure that money in the bank would set them free, free to travel, free to escape from disadvantages, free to exercise their talents and realize their desires." Well, that was the creed of many, but what do we think now, in this catastrophic world, about the adequacy of that? Money in the bank setting us free? If someone here thinks that a preacher is prejudiced, let that layman preach my sermon for me. If we are to have a free world we must get back to "the absolutely stupendous interpretation of life and history that Christianity offers."

Come further now and consider that in this matter we Christians are fortunate because our whole faith centers in a fact. Jesus Christ is a fact. He did actually live. That incarnation of all the best that we can mean by the Divine did walk the earth. To call him an ideal is to get started at the wrong end. He is first of all a realistic, stubborn, irremovable fact, that from the time they crucified him men have tried to get rid of and cannot.

If someone says, Yes, but still we know so little directly about him, the Gospels are so overlaid with the thinking of the first-century church, that the original likeness of Jesus is difficult to recover, I answer: To be sure! All New Testament scholars know that. In the Gospels we do not so much see Jesus directly; rather we see him as he impressed and influenced those first disciples. We have to look at him through their eyes and understand him in terms of what he did to them. But when one stops to consider that, how amazing it is!

Helen of Troy was so beautiful that the Greeks and Trojans fought a long war because of her. Yet read Homer's *Iliad* through and you will find no direct description of what Helen looked like. Scarcely a single word of that! All we know about Helen's beauty is put in terms of the way she affected people. Once when she walked upon the walls of Troy a group of old men sat by the gate and watched her pass, and Homer writes that as they saw her they said one to another: "Small blame is it that Trojans and well-greaved Achaians should for such a woman long time suffer hardships; marvellously like is she to the immortal goddesses to look upon." That is Homer's way of telling us how lovely Helen was. She made even old men feel that.

Now, in the Gospels that is the way Jesus' greatness is presented—in terms of what he did to people. His influence fell on Peter, James and John, plain fishermen, or on some woman taken in adultery, and see what happened! Reading the Gospels is like watching the sun rise, not by looking at the sun but by seeing the way it lights up everything it shines upon, transfiguring with glory the commonest bush it touches. One knows from what happens to the landscape that it cannot be an ordinary lamp; it must be the sun. So one sees Jesus in the gospels as he transfigures the lives upon whom his influence falls. Moreover, that effect of Jesus has never stopped. Wherever he has come and been genuinely welcomed, something transfiguring has happened. And now he stands in the midst of this modern world, still an inescapable fact, so that a friend of mine recently exclaimed, "A being who nineteen hundred years after his death can cause a civilization to question its own foundations is no insignificant Jewish carpenter."

My fellow Christians, our world faces now a prodigious choice: Christ or antichrist. Whose ideas shall dominate the world? Whose philosophy of life shall master the minds of our children and create the civilization in which they shall live? Christ or antichrist? They both are facts—not ideals merely but facts—one or the other of them representing the eternal truth about ourselves and this universe and its God. Mankind as a whole confronts the inescapable necessity of choosing, and so too we must choose, one by one. Can anyone here say that he honestly thinks it is not Christ but antichrist who has the right to say, "Ye shall know the truth, and the truth shall make you free"?

This, then, is what we mean by saying that it is not enough to have a private religion of one's own. The sun is my private affair, making my personal life possible, but it is more than that. It is a cosmic fact, everlastingly there whether I make it my private affair or not. Of such quality are the great affirmations of Christian faith. God is; Christ is his revealer; man is the child of the Eternal Spirit; there is an eternal purpose which he purposed in Christ; all men are members one of another; love is the law of life—such are the basic realities, says the New Testament.

To be sure, someone here may be fearful that this talk about a renaissance of doctrine means returning to the old slavery of dogmatic creeds. No! This sermon is preached to liberals, by a liberal whose intellectual liberty is a prized possession. The acknowledgment of religious truth is no more imprisoning than the acknowledgment of scientific truth. Indeed, I ask you, is the acceptance of these great affirmations of the Christian faith enslaving? Is it not, as Jesus said, the most liberating experience the soul of man can know? Look at what happens to the world when the opposite philosophy is accepted. It is antichrist, not Christ, who enslaves men.

Something important might take place in this listening congregation now. Conversion has commonly been interpreted in emotional terms, and we may not underrate the significance of those overturns in human personality that come with a floodtide of feeling. But some of us need to experience a conversion whose major element is intellectual. The great examples of conversion in the church have taken place in men and women who felt that in Christ they were confronting reality for the first time in their lives. Remember Keats' lines:

> Then felt I like some watcher of the skies
>   When a new planet swims into his ken;
> Or like stout Cortez when with eagle eyes
>   He star'd at the Pacific . . .

So! Brought face to face with a new fact, confronted for the first time with an everlasting truth, to which we must subject ourselves—that is a transfiguring experience. So may the Christian faith come to some life here, saying, "Ye shall know the truth, and the truth shall make you free."

When God Becomes Real

"BLESSED are the pure in heart," said Jesus, "for they shall see God." That is to say, to the pure in heart the Divine shall be vitally real. Whatever else this familiar beatitude does, it carries us deep into the Master's own experience. The Divine was a vivid Fact to him. He was an ethical teacher and a prophet of social righteousness, but he was more than that. He was a religious reformer and a specialist in human friendship, but all such things, however important, were like planets swung by and lighted from a central sun—God was real to him. From the time when as a boy in the temple he said to his parents, "Wist ye not that I must be about my Father's business?" until on the Cross he said, "Father, into thy hands I commend my spirit," the Divine was real to him.

The consequences have been astounding. We date all events on earth from the time of his coming and even H. G. Wells says that "his is easily the dominant figure in history." That is astounding—especially to anyone who has been in the country where he lived, has visited the little village where he grew up, has sensed the poverty of it all, the slim chance he had, the few years he lived, the bitter enemies he made, the unpromising followers he gathered. It is astonishing that he should be the dominant figure in history. He knew nothing about our modern science. He never invented anything. He never wrote a book.

He had no wealth, no prestige, little formal education. When still a young man, he died on Calvary; and who then could have guessed that history would even mention him in her footnotes? Yet he has become the dominant figure in history! Whatever other explanations may be given, this central fact should not be forgotten; here at least was one son of man to whom the Divine was vividly real. He did not simply believe in God or have opinions about God. Multitudes of people do that. God to him was a genuine, vitally experienced Fact, and his beatitude is autobiography: "Blessed are the pure in heart; for they shall see God."

This beatitude intimately concerns the religious problem of multitudes of us. The trouble with many of us is not that we think God untrue but that we find him unreal. It is one thing to believe in God, as almost all of us do; it is another thing to confront him as an inescapable reality.

Indeed, in any realm it is one kind of experience to believe in anything and it is another kind of experience altogether to find it real. We all believed in love before we fell in love ourselves. We had read the story of Ivanhoe and Rowena. We knew Romeo and Juliet. We had read Mrs. Browning's "Sonnets from the Portuguese." We believed in love. Then one day we fell in love ourselves, fell profoundly and abidingly in love, so that this thing in which we always had believed became real to us, became light and life and power in us. In any realm it is one thing to believe and another thing to see.

So far as faith in God is concerned, I am speaking for practically all of us today when I say that we are not disbelievers. We could as easily think that musical notes fortuitously fell together into a Chopin nocturne as to believe that this vast, amazing universe accidentally created and arranged itself. If someone protests that this universe is not at all like a Chopin nocturne, that it is terrific, ruthless, full of discord, I answer: Say your worst about this universe, say even that it is like these cacophonies with which our modern orchestras sometimes assail our ears; emphasize its disharmonies, tragedies, cruelties, often hard to stand and difficult to see head or tail to; nevertheless, with all the mystery, we do face here creative Power issuing in a law-abiding world which a physicist like Jeans rightly says "seems to be nearer to a great thought than to a great machine," and which before our very eyes flowers out in personalities and spiritual values and social possibilities.

No, we are not atheists, but that is about as far as some of us ever get. God is not real to us. Own up, my friends! To be sure, once in a while, when some great experience stirs us to the depths, the Divine may be real, but, for the most part, to multitudes of people God is only a matter of opinion and belief.

Let us clarify our thought now as to what we mean by having anything real to us. For one thing, it implies emotional vividness. Do we believe, for example, that nature, with her mountains, seas and lakes, her forests and her flowers, is beautiful? Of course we do. Any straggler down the street, buttonholed for consent to that opinion, would give it. But if we ask whether the beauty of nature is real to us, that is another matter. In the vast canyons of our city's streets, between these towering walls of brick and stone, some of us go week after week and never think of nature. We do not see the stars by night nor the new crescent of the moon amid the glare of our electric lights. We do not have, like Wordsworth among his lakes and mountains,

> that inward eye
> Which is the bliss of solitude.

It is one thing to believe that nature is beautiful and it is another thing to feel it, to have it emotionally vivid. So deep is the difference in religion. "I believe in God the Father Almighty"— that is an opinion, a belief. "Enter into thine inner chamber, and having shut thy door, pray to thy Father who is in secret"— that is finding God real.

Again, whatever is real to us, being thus emotionally vivid, becomes confidently assured. In our modern Protestantism there is much vagueness and doubt, and the reason is not difficult to discover. There are only two ways in which any man finds certitude and confidence in religion. Either he does it by accepting as infallible some external authority, like the pope, or else he himself inwardly has a convincing awareness of God.

In his *Spiritual Exercises,* intended for the training of Jesuits, Ignatius Loyola says that "we ought always to be ready to believe that what seems to us white is black, if the hierarchical Church so defines it." If a man is thus willing to put out his own eyes and trust himself to the absolute guidance of another, he can have that sort of confident assurance which such external authority provides. When, however, people like ourselves have surrendered *that,* when we will not accept our beliefs from anyone's infallible say-so, then only one way is left in which certitude and confidence in religion can be achieved. We ourselves inwardly must have a convincing awareness of God that makes him indubitably real.

Let it be frankly said that some Roman Catholics, with their assurance which rests back upon trust in an infallible authority, are religiously better off than many Protestants are. Many Protestants are only halfway Protestant. That is to say, they have gone far enough to throw off the authority of ecclesiastical dogma, but they have not gone far enough to secure that certitude, confidence and therefore power which come from a deep, inward awareness of the Divine which makes him unquestionably sure. Ask some of us what we think about the beauty of a true home and you know the flaming certainty with which we would answer you. No doubt or vagueness would afflict our confidence. A true home is the most beautiful relationship on earth. We are not taking that on anybody's say-so. No pope by ex-cathedra utterance persuaded us of that. We are sure of that because we have vitally, personally, vividly perceived it. What could we not do on this earth with a few people to whom the Divine was thus real!

Moreover, whatever is real to us, being thus emotionally vivid and confidently assured, becomes morally controlling. Be sure of this: wherever anything happens on this earth for the good of man, something has become real to somebody. From the time we first had knowledge that the earth is round, we all have held beliefs and opinions about the North Pole, but they never did anything to us. Then came a man named Peary, to whom that whole matter was so vivid that he could say, "For more than a score of years that point on the earth's surface had been the object of my every effort." You see, it is not the things we theoretically believe that make the difference so much as it is the things which are real to us. In our present situation we do not need people with mere beliefs and opinions about social justice and humanity. There are multitudes of such. We need people to whom social justice and humaneness are so real that, despite the clamorous selfishness which is in the heart of all of us, they cannot help living for them.

Here, alas! is the source of hypocrisy: a man says he believes in one thing when another thing is real to him. I believe in Christianity, says this woman. Yet look at her! Anyone can see that not Christian living but social ambition is her dominant motive. She is a social climber. Above anything else on earth she wants to walk in what she regards as the preferred circles of the town. She is trying to crash the gate. Let her repeat all the creeds in Christendom; what is real to her is something else.

I believe in Christ, says this man, but look at him! He is a preacher who is not honestly interested to speak the truth as he sees it but is anxious rather to curry popular favor, or he is a businessman who is playing the money-making game with whatever slickness and ruthlessness he thinks he can get away with. Let him go on saying, I believe in Christ; something else is real to him.

The source of hypocrisy lies here, that a man says, I believe in a high thing, when a low thing is vivid to his eyes. Today, therefore, I am not talking about our beliefs. Belief can be a profound matter, involving the vitalities we are stressing now—"Believe on the Lord Jesus Christ, and thou shalt be saved" means that—but often our beliefs lie loosely about on the surface of our lives. I am talking about our realities, emotionally vivid, confidently assured, morally controlling.

If this is what we mean by having anything real to us, let us look again at this beatitude! It tells us that if a man is to have the Divine real to him a condition must be fulfilled: only the pure in heart can see God. When one stops to think of it, that is a strange condition to lay down as a prerequisite to seeing God. No one of us would have dreamed of saying anything like that. We would have said, If a man is to know God he must have the large grasp of a philosophic mind, but we never would have thought of talking about a pure heart. Indeed, if we are looking for God off somewhere among the stars or are trying to find him at the end of a metaphysical argument, then for the life of me I cannot see what purity of heart has to do with that. But suppose we are trying to find God where Jesus looked for him. Jesus put a little child before his disciples and said, "Of such is the kingdom of heaven." To find the Divine in a child takes a clean heart, clean from sophistication and cynicism and unkindness. Jesus went out into nature and said, "Consider the lilies of the field. . . . Solomon in all his glory was not arrayed like one of these. . . . God doth so clothe the grass." To find God in the grass takes a clean heart.

Jesus ran upon Peter, James and John, ordinary men in whom commonplace eyes would never have seen anything but commonplace things, and Jesus discovered in them divine possibilities and brought them out. To find divine things in common people—that takes a clean heart, clean from scorn and contemptuousness and derision. Jesus went out into a social situation full of injustice and into an ecclesiastical situation full of conventionality and corruption, where acquiescence on his part would have been safe and easy, and he heard a divine challenge to service. To hear the Divine calling to us out of a social situation where personality is being hurt takes a clean heart. On the night before he was crucified Jesus went out into the garden of Gethsemane, and held there a tryst with the Divine that the world has never yet been able to forget. That took a clean heart.

You see, Jesus was not doing what we constantly do—looking for God somewhere off among the stars or trying to find him at the end of an argument. He was seeing God—do we get that?— *seeing* him in children and nature and plain people, in ordinary situations and in opportunities for service. My soul! Stop arguing about God for a moment and sit down before this towering fact that the real God takes eyes to see.

Of course, the real *anything* takes eyes to see. Blessed are the pure in heart: for they shall see—you could stop the beatitude there. Blessed are the pure in heart: for they shall see friendship and beauty and love and goodness. All such things take eyes to see. The real Sistine Madonna does not lie at the end of an argument; it takes eyes to see. A great friendship does not lie at the end of an argument. You can argue concerning it but it takes eyes to see deeply into another's soul.

I stood once on a noble slope of the Alps on one of those priceless days when the autumnal coloring was just beginning to appear and, wrapped in silence amid the majesty of the mountains, I saw two of my countrywomen steaming up beside me. One called out, "We have heard that there is a view somewhere up here. Where is it?" What was the use of arguing? There it was but it took eyes to see. It takes eyes to see even scientific truth. Recall those notable words of Thomas Huxley: "Sit down," he said, "sit down before fact as a little child, be prepared to give up every preconceived notion, follow humbly wherever and to whatever abysses nature leads, or you shall learn nothing." To be sure! To have eyes pure from prejudice, clean from the astigmatism of preconceived opinions—without *that* nobody ever found scientific truth.

You people here, especially in this academic environment, forever arguing about God, I do not ask you to stop your arguments but I do beg of you to go a long way beyond them. Suppose you did discover the God whom you are looking for at the end of your arguments, what good would that do? Multitudes of people have argued themselves into believing in God and then have discovered that it has made little difference to their lives. They did not go on to see this deeper matter:

> . . . Earth's crammed with heaven,
> And every common bush afire with God:
> But only he who sees, takes off his shoes.

I venture that more than once some of us have emerged from a subway kiosk in some unfamiliar portion of this city and have found ourselves all turned around. The trouble did not lie in our beliefs. We still believed that north was north and south was south, and our opinions about east and west were orthodox. That, however, did not save the situation. What good did our beliefs do until we could make them real to us? And some of us have stood still for fairly five minutes until we could make ourselves *see* what we *believed.*

In the religious life that is one of the meanings of prayer. It means being still, for at least five minutes, until the great faiths and values which make life worth living become true to our eyes.

Some of you may have been feeling that this sermon is a long way off from the hectic hurly-burly of our distracted time but, my friend, it well may be that you, who are thinking that, are the one person of all others needing this truth. You are all turned around. Yes, you are! It is easy enough to be *that* in ordinary times. It is easier now. We believe in God. Yes! We believe in the major propositions of an inherited Christianity. Yes! But we are all turned around. The spiritual values which give a man his direction, so that he knows which way he ought to go in a confused time, are not real to us. We have been neglecting those exercises out of which come eyes that see.

This is the essence of the matter, that there is no religion which amounts to much except that which is to be found in people to whom the Divine is thus real. The older I grow the less interest I have in any other kind. Across the lines of prejudice that separate church from church and religion from religion, my heart goes out to all those men and women of every creed and clime in whom this authentic sign appears, that the Divine is real to them. From Gandhi in India and Kagawa in Japan to men like Phillips Brooks in our own tradition, these have been the flaming souls who amid the dust and ashes of religious conventionality have made religion a living fire. Give us enough people to whom in personal character and social relationships the Divine is real, and we can lift humanity yet out of its slough of despond.

Well, what is real to us? For, my friends, nothing beside that can ever be any man's vital religion.

Conservative and Liberal
Temperaments in Religion

L ET us set over against each other this morning two passages
of Scripture which convey an antithetical message about
what used to be a live problem in religion. Both passages concern the sacred ark which Moses made of shittim wood, which
contained the tables of the Law and which the ancient Hebrews
called "the ark of God." How venerable it was in their sight
one feels when, for example, one reads Joshua 7:6: "Joshua rent
his clothes, and fell to the earth upon his face before the ark of
the Lord until the evening." There was the appropriate place
for Joshua to pray. There God, so he thought, particularly dwelt.
And one has only to read the subsequent history of that ark,
when David carried it up to Zion, and Solomon put it into the
Holy of Holies as Israel's most precious talisman, to see how
indissolubly those early Hebrews associated their faith in God
with that sacred chest.

Let nearly six hundred years pass by, however, and we are
opening the Bible at the prophecies of Jeremiah. In his third
chapter and sixteenth verse he is talking about this same ark but
in a tone of voice how different! "In those days, says the Lord,
they shall no more say, The ark of the covenant of the Lord.
It shall not come to mind, or be remembered, or missed; it shall
not be made again."

Here, obviously, is a clear contrast. On the one side, Joshua has his faith in God identified with that sacred ark. Where the ark goes he thinks God goes. But here, on the other side, is Jeremiah, ardent prophet of the living God, for whom that ark is meaningless. He is glad that it is gone. He wishes it no more to be remembered or rebuilt.

We call our generation a time of religious transition. We say that everything is in flux, but in a sense every generation has been a time of religious transition and here in the Bible itself we see so typical an example of changing faith that it may have a worth-while message to bring to us. For here too the people associated their religion with one of its particular historic exhibitions: a holy ark. Around that ark their faith gathered, about it their enthusiasms burned. When they thought religion they thought ark. Here, however, is a prophet of the living God who towers higher than all the generations that venerated the ark, a man who became a forerunner of the Christ and a sharer of his spirit. He has no use for the ark at all. He is thanking God that it is gone forever.

Nobody who knows anything about human nature can suppose that such a change took place easily. There must have been the same distress of mind, doubt, lost faith, and hurt bewilderment of spiritual life that comes in every time of religious transition. May it not be that we have here a typical instance of changing faith so far removed from our passions and prejudices that we may look at it coolly and objectively and find light upon the problems that concern us?

One comment immediately suggests itself as we ponder the significance of this ancient incident. The idea that the Bible is a unanimous book upon one level is quite incredible to anybody

who knows the Bible at all. Open the Book of Psalms and you
will find David, who in his time was accounted a man after
God's own heart, represented as roundly cursing his enemies:

> Grant that his children be fatherless,
>   And that his wife be a widow.
> Up and down may his children go begging,
>   Expelled from their desolate home.
> May all that he owneth be seized by the creditor,
>   May strangers plunder the fruits of his toil.
> May none extend to him kindness,
>   Or pity his fatherless children.

So cursed the Psalmist. But when one turns the pages and comes
to the place where the Master speaks, how different is the tone!
"Ye have heard that it was said, Thou shalt love thy neighbor,
and hate thine enemy: but I say unto you, Love your enemies,
and pray for them that persecute you." You cannot iron those
two passages out to one level. The Bible throughout is the record
of religious movement, in constant process of transition, and our
morning's incident is only one illustration of a universal fact
about Scripture: wherever you get an ark, organize your religion
about it, try to settle down with it, a growing faith says, Move
on! and prophets of the living God cry out that the ark should
no longer be remembered or remade.

A second comment grows out of this incident: religion, on the
one side, and, on the other, particular exhibitions of it like an
ark, are not the same thing. Arks pass away but religion remains.
Should we go down to Joshua in the flat marl plain at Gilgal
where he lies before the ark and try to explain to him that some
day folk will come devoutly loving God, deeply believing in him,
who will have no care for that ark at all, how difficult it would

be for Joshua to understand! Real religion without that ark? How can he imagine that?

It is easy for us in retrospect to see that Joshua would be mistaken, but, nevertheless, we commonly make the same mistake. We identify Christian faith with some particular expression of it until we find it difficult to think that anyone can have genuine Christian life who does not share our veneration for that special custom, ritual or belief.

My grandmother said to me once that if she could not believe that the whale swallowed Jonah she would lose her Christianity. Hers was a beautiful spiritual life whose secret sources were deep hid with Christ in God, and yet she thought that spiritual life was indissolubly associated with a special whale swallowing a special man. Of course it was not. Of course that was an artificial adhesion. All of us who knew her knew that her radiant and luminous Christian spirit was not necessarily related with any whale.

What your whale is you probably know. We all have them: those points of view in theology, those special expressions of religion, that have been precious in our spiritual experience so that we are tempted to identify real religion with them until it is difficult to think that anyone can have real religion without them. It is a great day, therefore, in a man's life when he sees that religion is greater than and is separable from these special exhibitions of it, as living water can be carried in many a receptacle to which we ourselves have not been accustomed.

In this regard religion is much like courtesy. Courtesy is an inward spirit, as religion is, easy to recognize, difficult to define, that expresses itself in many forms. The courteous American and the courteous Japanese have the same spirit but they express it differently, as any traveler in Japan must see. Who would insist that a Jew going into a synagogue and keeping his hat on is less courteous than a Christian going into church and taking off his hat, when through two different customs the same reverence is expressed? He who deals with many groups of people must learn to discern courtesy below many forms.

Such discernment, however, which is not difficult in the matter of courtesy, comes very hard in the matter of religion. When, for example, all Western Christendom was Roman Catholic and Protestantism began, how hard it was to think that you could have a genuine Christian life without the old embodiments in which it had been expressed! Real religion without the mass, without the veneration of the blessed Virgin and the saints? Yet when Protestantism, like Catholicism, began to produce its own great souls, its prophets and apostles, its martyrs, saints and mystics, then it became plain that real spiritual life is separable from those ancient arks. When, then, Protestantism began building its own arks, as religion always does—its creeds and liturgies, its rituals and sacraments—the Quakers came. They did not like creeds. Especially, they did not like rituals and sacraments. Could there be genuine Christian life on such a basis? You know how hard that was for the old-time Protestants to see. But when souls like Whittier had begun to live as well as sing,

> O Sabbath rest by Galilee!
> O calm of hills above!
> Where Jesus knelt to share with thee
> The silence of eternity,
> Interpreted by love,

there was no use denying that that was bona fide Christianity, deeply rooted in Christ.

It is a great hour for a man, then, when he perceives that

religion is like the sea, that it flows into many different bays, taking a different shape in each and getting a different name. That does not mean, to be sure, that one must think one bay is as good as another. One bay may be very broad and deep, where the navies of the world could ride; another bay may be small and shallow, choked with marsh and mud and blockaded by sandbars. But the wise man will discern the same sea in all of them and a wise man will never identify the sea with any of them. For the bay may grow or dwindle, may flourish or be deserted, but the sea remains.

That is the central message of the morning: from Joshua to Jeremiah what a change! how many alterations! Joshua's ark had gone! But religion had not. Religion had thrived and grown.

Obviously, this morning's truth has practical bearing on a very lively modern problem—the way in which our two temperaments, the conservative and the liberal, behave themselves in matters of religion. Some of us are temperamentally conservative and some of us are temperamentally liberal. You who still love Gilbert and Sullivan's operas remember the song:

> That every boy and every gal
> That's born into the world alive
> Is either a little Liberal
> Or else a little Conservative!

That is true, not simply in politics; it is true in religion also and, moreover, it is a good thing that it is true. We need both those temperaments.

It takes two hands on a clock to make it tell time. One goes fast and the other goes slow, but it takes both of them to make a good clock. So it takes the liberal and the conservative temperaments to make a good country and a good church, and the most balanced and wise leader is the man who has both elements in him. It may be that this morning's message has something to say to both these temperaments by way of wise warning and good counsel.

First, let us address ourselves to the conservatives. Consider what it means to the conservative temperament that Joshua's ark was overpassed but that in Jeremiah spiritual life flowed out into forms much nobler and more beautiful than Joshua knew. It is always difficult for a conservative Joshua, with his ark, to believe that a man like Jeremiah may come without his ark and, not missing it, may yet fly higher and plunge deeper into real religion. That is the tragedy of the conservative temperament when it goes wrong.

Remember what the conservative Athenians, for example, called Socrates. They said he was an atheist. Yet read Plato's *Phaedo* and see how much of an atheist he was—one of the great believers in God and immortality, one of the high spirits in the history of religion. Only, he did play Jeremiah to their Joshua and say, The ark is gone. And so they made him drink the hemlock.

So Jesus laid his hands upon the Sabbath laws of his time. They were very sacred. Religion had hallowed them. And the ardent partisans of conservative Judaism said that he had a devil, that he was a blasphemer of God, and in the name of religion cried "Crucify him" against the one who was religion's transcendent expositor. That is the tragedy of the conservative temperament when it goes wrong. It finds difficulty in recognizing the reailty and beauty and power of a real religion when it turns up in new forms with fresh methods of expression.

Some time ago I ordered a book from a bookstore. I was familiar with it. I had seen it before. When, therefore, I undid the package I was vexed. See, I said, this is not the book I ordered; they have made a mistake and wasted time. Then I looked again and saw that I was wrong. It was the same book but it was in a new binding. And as I turned its pages I recognized that, for all its unfamiliar appearance, the old delight was waiting for me still. That is perhaps the deepest thing that the conservative temperament needs to cultivate: insight to perceive old truth in new bindings.

Of course, the psychological fact that causes this difficulty with the conservative temperament is obvious. Religion makes sacred everything it touches. Religion, for example, associates itself with a world view, like the flatness of the earth or fiat creation. Religion twines its tendrils around that world view, hallows it, makes it sacred, so that, when science utterly shifts the scene, religion only reluctantly gives up its hold on the sacredness of the old view or, it may be, does not give it up at all. Within my recollection Voliva of Zion City was using the radio to tell the world that the earth is flat.

Or religion may associate itself with a language like Latin, in which the Roman rituals used to be performed. Then times change, new vernacular tongues come in, all the business of the world is done in living languages. Still the ancient church worships in Latin, as many religions worship in old and sometimes dead tongues.

Very powerful is this preservative spirit of religion that hallows everything it touches, so that in Jerusalem today you can find Jews who would not for the world set foot upon the sacred platform where their ancient temple stood, because they think that underneath it somewhere this very ark that Moses made and Joshua prayed before is waiting, and they would not profane the spot where it rests.

What your ark is I do not know. We all have one. It may be some special doctrine, some denominational peculiarity, some bit of ritual, some miracle in history; it may be fiat creation or the Virgin Birth or baptism by immersion or a special theory of the Atonement. Such things may have been very precious in your experience. Your religion has twined itself around them. No considerate man, no matter how clearly he disagreed with your opinions, would speak a disrespectful word about them. Let us practice the fine art of reverencing each other's reverences. But what one would say is this: beware of your judgments on people who do not venerate your ark. Beware how you suspect that they cannot have genuine Christian life without your ark. You say you want to keep the faith. Aye, but keeping the faith is one thing and keeping the ark is another. Jeremiah kept the faith; he carried it out into a new day; he lifted it higher than it ever had been lifted before; he became a forerunner of the Christ. He kept the faith but he did not keep the ark. Keeping the ark would not have helped; it would have hindered. Whatever may be your ark, and in this regard we all have our conservatisms—that is the message of the morning to the conservative temperament.

Perhaps the morning's message to the liberal temperament is even more important. Think what it means to the liberal that it took a man like Jeremiah, the finest exhibition, I think, of personal religion in our history before Jesus, successfully and helpfully to overpass that ark.

This business of reforming religion and getting rid of old symbols and old ideas that impede the progress of religion is a good deal more serious matter than many liberals seem to think, and this is the gist of the matter: nothing can reform religion except religion—finer, deeper, more devout, more spiritual, more creative religion. Nothing else can reform religion but that. If the world is to be any better because Joshua is overpassed, it will take a Jeremiah to do it.

You see, there are two ways of getting rid of an ark. One is to smash it, to say: That ark is nothing but superstition, away with it! But it is not true that that ark is nothing but superstition. It is more than that. It at least is a trellis around which some very lovely things have twined themselves. It is to many a symbol of the best spiritual life they know up to date. If liberalism can do nothing else but smash arks, it may succeed merely in leaving the spiritual life of a whole generation bereft, without trellises to twine around, without symbols to express itself through. If helpfully the ark is to be overpassed, that must be done by men and women who possess in themselves religion deep, fine, devout, creative.

Some time since, a housewife, wanting to clean stains from her tablecloth, tried to do it with nitric acid. The experiment worked but there was a serious drawback to it. For the nitric acid not only took away the stains; it took away the tablecloth. Some of our theological liberalism has been doing that. Contemporary religion, it says, is soiled; it is stained; it needs to be reformed. I do not see how any man with half an eye can doubt it. But nitric acid will not get us anywhere. That not only takes away the evils of religion; alas, too often it takes away religion too.

Here in our morning's incident, therefore, we have a clear indication of the right method. Go down to the Gilgal plain and watch Joshua as he bows before that ark. What an odd

way to pray to God, as though he inhabited a sacred chest!
Away with that kind of prayer! one would say. But when you
come to Jeremiah he is not spending much time in saying, Away
with that, or any other, kind of prayer. He is most positively
praying. He is praying with a depth and a height that Joshua
never could have imagined: "O Lord, my strength, and my
stronghold, and my refuge in the day of affliction." He is reforming religion with religion.

Or come down to the plain of Gilgal again and think how
Joshua conceived God housed in a sacred ark, so that where the
ark went God went. How pathetic a theology! Away with that
superstition! But when you come to Jeremiah you see that he
is not wasting much time saying, Away with any theology! He
is lifting up positively a new conception of God so much higher,
so much deeper, so much finer than Joshua could have dreamed,
that anyone with spiritual discernment must see it. Listen to
Jeremiah's God: "Can any hide himself in secret places that I
shall not see him? saith the Lord. Do not I fill heaven and
earth?" That is reforming religion with religion.

Or go back once more to that Gilgal plain and watch Joshua
pray. What is he praying for? He is praying because he is
angry, because yesterday his warriors went up to Ai to sack the
town and were defeated. He wants to know what is the matter.
He wants tomorrow to send those warriors back and massacre,
as he did at last, man and woman and child without mercy.
Away with such superstition! one would cry. But when you
come to Jeremiah you see how it must be done. Listen to him
positively talking about war: "I cannot hold my peace; because
thou hast heard, O my soul, the sound of the trumpet, the
alarm of war."

Nothing can reform religion except religion. In every realm

that principle runs true. What a marvelous renaissance in art came from Cimabue and Giotto, through Raphael. They broke away from the stiff unreality of Byzantine painting and created an art of unsurpassed beauty. But they did it by the positive production of loveliness. They reformed art with more art, finer, more resplendent, more true to life.

We liberals should not miss this lesson. Nothing but religion can reform religion. Intellectual dilettantes cannot do it. Undedicated Athenians, spending their time "in nothing else, but either to tell or to hear some new thing," cannot do it. Only men and women who really know what vital religion is can do it. You say, Religion ought to be reformed. So say I. But when we say it, let us look humbly into our own souls. How much better do you think the world would really be if it had no other quality of spiritual life than that which we possess?

This is the upshot of the discussion, then, that we people of conservative and liberal temperaments would better make up our minds to work together. We need each other and at our deepest and our best we both want the same thing: vital, personal religion of the kind that produces character and sends out unselfish servants to build the kingdom of righteousness in this world.

Consider the significance of this simple fact, that we Christians are separated by our creeds and rituals but are united by our prayers and hymns. Go into a church and listen to the creed and how often you will say, I cannot repeat that creed; that church is not for me. Go into a church and observe the ritual and say, I cannot feel the significance of that liturgy; that church is not for me. We are divided by our creeds and rituals. But because they come from the nethersprings of life we are united by our prayers and hymns. Pick up any great compilation of Christian prayers. Where do they come from? They come from everywhere, from Paul and St. Augustine, from Thomas à Kempis and George Matheson. They come from all ages of the church and all kinds of Christians. There are the deeps of religion that underlie division.

It is because of that, I presume, that our hymnal is the most catholic element in Christianity. There we sing with a Fundamentalist,

> Rock of Ages, cleft for me,
> Let me hide myself in Thee,

and with a Unitarian,

> Nearer, my God, to thee,
> Nearer to thee.

There we sing with a Roman Catholic,

> Lead, kindly Light, amid the encircling gloom,

and with a Quaker,

> Dear Lord and Father of mankind,
> Forgive our feverish ways.

Then we go far back across the centuries and paraphrase the ancient Psalms,

> The king of love my shepherd is,
> Whose goodness faileth never,

and we come down to sing with contemporary saints,

> Spirit of God, descend upon my heart.

If, then, you ask what a true liberalism is, I should say that it is one that pays little attention to the arks that divide, but cares with all its heart about the religion that unites us. Such religion has issued in may arks in the past and will issue in many more; out of it have come our theologies and rituals and were they to be wiped off the earth today many more would spring from the same source. Such religion is the blue sky behind the passing clouds, it is the deep sea beneath the transient waves. For here, too, what is seen, the outward embodiment, is temporal, but what is unseen, the life that is hid with Christ in God, is eternal.

The Importance of Doubting
Our Doubts

In the vocabulary of religion the word "doubt" has a bad significance. Have you ever heard a preacher use it in a favorable sense? Faith is the great word. Faith is the victory that overcomes the world, and is not doubt its chief enemy? So the word "doubt" has been exiled to religion's semantic doghouse.

But that does not solve the problem. Once more today I feel what I commonly feel when I face worshiping congregations. You look so pious. You are so reverent. You listen so respectfully to Scripture and anthem. You sing so earnestly the resounding hymns. Yet I know and you know that in every life here is something else which our worship does not express—doubts, questions, uncertainties, skepticisms. Every one of us, facing the Christian faith, must honestly say what the man in the Gospel story said to Jesus: "Lord, I believe; help thou mine unbelief." Especially, in these days, so disturbing to placid, docile faith about God and man, how applicable are the Bishop's words in Browning's poem:

> With me, faith means perpetual unbelief,
> Kept quiet like the snake 'neath Michael's foot,
> Who stands calm just because he feels it writhe.

Concerning this problem, which in one way or another we all face, I offer two preliminary observations. First, doubt is not a "snake"; the capacity to doubt is one of man's noblest powers. Look at our world today and see the innumerable beliefs and practices, from communism up and down, which ought to be doubted! The great servants of our race have been distinguished by the fact that in the face of universally accepted falsehoods they dared stand up and cry: I doubt that! Without the capacity to doubt there could be no progress—only docile, unquestioning acceptance of the status quo and its established dogmatisms.

Think of the scientific realm! The earth is flat, the sun circles round it—when such ideas were everywhere accepted, a few bravely dared to disbelieve them. Every scientific advance has started with skepticism. When we think of the scientific pioneers we emphasize their faith, their affirmative belief in new ideas and possibilities. Right! But in the experience of the pioneers themselves their first poignant struggle, their initial critical venture, centered in perilous and daring disbelief. Galileo was right when he called doubt the father of discovery.

But, someone says, when we turn from science to religion, we want faith—faith in God, in Christ, in the human soul. Of course we want faith! But anyone who thinks he can achieve great faith without exercising his God-given capacity to doubt, is oversimplifying the problem. Jesus himself was a magnificent doubter. Wild ideas of a war-making Messiah who would overthrow Rome were prevalent in his time. He doubted them. "An eye for an eye and a tooth for a tooth" was the true law, they said. He doubted it. He saw men trusting in long prayers, broad phylacteries, rigid Sabbath rules, dietary laws as essential to true religion, and he doubted them all. He saw men believing in ancient traditions just because they were ancient, and he poured his skepticism on such reactionaries: "It was said unto them of old time, but I say unto you." Samaritans are an inferior race was the popular idea, but he scorned it; a good Samaritan, he said, is better than a bad priest. We are saved by Jesus' faith, we say. Yes, but just as truly as any scientific pioneer did, he reached his faith through his daring doubts. My friends, we sing the praises of the great believers. So do I! But who can worthily express our unpayable indebtedness to the brave doubters, who in perilous times, when false ideas dominated men's minds and spoiled their lives, saved the day with their courageous disbelief? Let us sing their praises too!

To someone here, struggling with this problem, I am saying first: Don't despise your capacity to doubt! Honor it! It is one of your noblest attributes.

My second preliminary observation is that the sturdiest faith has always come out of the struggle with doubt. There are only two ways in which we can possess Christian faith. One is to inherit it, borrow it, swallow it without question, take it over as we do the cut of our clothes without thinking about it. Some here may be able to do that, but your faith then is not really *yours*. You never fought for it. As one student said: "Being a Methodist, just because your parents were, is like wearing a secondhand hat that does not fit." No! Great faith, if it is really to be one's very own, always has to be fought for.

One who does not understand this, does not understand the Bible. It is a book of faith, we say. To be sure it is! But it is also a book filled with the struggles of men wrestling with their doubts and unbelief. Listen to Gideon crying, "If the Lord is with us, why then has all this befallen us?" Listen to the Psalmist:

> My tears have been my food day
> and night,

While they continually say unto me,
Where is thy God?

Listen to Job complaining to God: "I cry unto thee, and thou
dost not answer me," or to Jeremiah calling God "a deceitful
brook" and "waters that fail," and crying, "Cursed be the day
on which I was born!"

The Bible only a book of faith? But listen to Ecclesiastes:
"Vanity of vanities, all is vanity. . . . That which befalleth the
sons of men befalleth beasts . . . as the one dieth, so dieth the
other; yea, they have all one breath; and man hath no pre-
eminence above the beasts." Indeed, listen to our Lord himself
on Calvary! He is quoting the twenty-second Psalm. He knows
it by heart: "My God, my God, why hast thou forsaken me?
Why art thou so far from helping me?" I am talking to someone here who is struggling with his doubts. The Bible is your
book, my friend. All its faith was hammered out on the hard
anvil of doubt.

The trouble is that most Christians know about the faith of
the great believers but not about their inner struggles. All Yale
men here, and many more of us too, remember William Lyon
Phelps. What a radiant Christian faith he had! But listen to him
in his autobiography: "My religious faith remains in possession
of the field only after prolonged civil war with my naturally
sceptical mind." That experience belongs in the best tradition of
the great believers. John Knox, the Scottish Reformer—what a
man of conviction! Yes, but remember that time when his soul
knew "anger, wrath and indignation, which it conceived against
God, calling all his promises in doubt." Increase Mather—that
doughty Puritan—what a man of faith! Yes, but read his diary
and run on entries like this: "Greatly molested with temptations
to atheism." Sing Luther's hymn, "A mighty fortress is our God,"

and one would suppose he never questioned his faith, but see him in other hours. "For more than a week," he wrote, "Christ was wholly lost. I was shaken by desperation and blasphemy against God."

I speak for the encouragement of someone here struggling with his unbelief. The noblest faith of the church has come out of that struggle. No man really possesses the Christian faith until he has fought for it. So Browning put it:

> The more of doubt, the stronger faith, I say,
> If faith o'ercomes doubt.

That brings us to the vital issue. How does faith overcome doubt?

Today I emphasize one central matter in the experience of the great believers: they went honestly through with their disbeliefs until at last they began to doubt their doubts. How important that process is! When it was first suggested that steamships could be built which would cross the ocean, multitudes were skeptical. One man proved it could not be done. He wrote a book proving that no steamship could carry enough fuel to keep its engines going across the ocean. Well, the first steamship that crossed the Atlantic and landed in New York Harbor carried a copy of that book. Ah, my skeptical disbeliever, you would have been a wiser man had you carried your doubt a little further until you doubted your doubts! I am preaching this sermon because I want someone here not to stop doubting, but to go through with his skepticism until he disbelieves his disbelief.

Let us apply this first to our faith in God! Someone here is struggling with doubts about God. Well, there are many ideas of God which ought to be doubted. The Bible itself progresses from one discarded idea of God to a nobler concept of him because men dared to doubt. But when it comes to surrendering belief in God and becoming an atheist, have you ever carried your doubts through to *that* conclusion? See where that lands you! No God! Nothing ultimately creative here except protons and electrons going it blind! All creation, as one atheist says, only "a curious accident in a backwater!" Everything explained by the chance collocation of physical elements! All the law-abiding order and beauty of the world, all the nobility of human character at its best, explained as though the physical letters of the alphabet had been blown together by a chance wind into the Thirteenth Chapter of First Corinthians! Christ himself and all he stands for—nothing, as it were, nothing but the physical notes of the musical scale tossed by purposeless winds until accidentally they fell together into the Ninth Symphony! Can you really believe that? Is not that utterly incredible?

In the United States today we face a strong trend back toward religious faith, and one reason, I think, lies in what we are saying now. Many in this last generation surrendered to skepticism, went through with it to its conclusion, until they began finding their disbelief unbelievable.

So Robert Louis Stevenson became a man of radiant faith, but he did not start that way. He started by calling the religion he was brought up in "the deadliest gag and wet-blanket that can be laid on man." He started by calling himself "a youthful atheist." Then, as he grew up, began what Gilbert Chesterton called his "first wild doubts of doubt." "The church was not right," wrote Stevenson, "but certainly not the antichurch either." " 'Tis a strange world," he said, "but there is a manifest God for those who care to look for him." Then at last he began talking about his "cast-iron faith." "Whether on the first of

January or the thirty-first of December," he wrote, "faith is a good word to end on." So he went through with his skepticism until he found his disbelief unbelievable.

I thank God now that that experience of Stevenson's was mine too. When I started for college my junior year, I told my mother that I was going to clear God out of the universe and begin all over to see what I could find. I could not swallow the Christian faith unquestioningly. I had to fight for it. And so it's mine! Every doubt raised against it, every question asked about it, I have faced often with agony of mind. I am not afraid of atheism; of all my disbeliefs I most certainly disbelieve that! And now in my elder years what a Christian of the last generation said I understand: "Who never doubted never half believed."

Let us apply this truth now not only to faith in God but to faith in Christ. For many people he is hard to believe in now. Too good to be true! Too idealistic to fit this naughty world! So the idea creeps in that believers are credulous, gullible, soft-headed, trusting this lovely Christ with his lovely ideas as "the way, the truth and the life." Often on university campuses one runs upon this idea that to believe in Christ is comforting—yes!—but it takes a credulous mind to do it in a world like this. To which I say: watch your step there! Again and again in history the shoe has been on the other foot. Not the believers in spiritual greatness, but the unbelievers have proved to be mistaken.

I thought of that when recently in Washington I stood before the Lincoln Memorial, saw again that noble figure seated there, and read on the carved stone the immortal words of the Gettysburg Address. A newspaper editor in Harrisburg, thirty-five miles away from Gettysburg, heard Lincoln's Gettysburg Address. Fall for that kind of stuff? Not he! He was no sucker! He was a hardheaded realist, he was! So he wrote this in his paper: "We pass over the silly remarks of the President; for the credit of the nation, we are willing that the veil of oblivion shall be dropped over them and that they shall no more be repeated or thought of." Ah, you fool, you stood in the presence of greatness, and you disbelieved! It is you who were blind. It is you, the skeptic, at whom the centuries will laugh till the end of time. You doubted Lincoln. Why didn't you think twice, until you doubted your doubts?

The older I grow the more I ponder Judas Iscariot. He came so near to *not* betraying Jesus. He was a loyal disciple. It took courage to join that little band, and Judas had it. Then doubts began. What kind of Messiah was this who refused violent revolution and talked about loving one's enemies? Was not this idealistic Jesus letting them down? So the doubts grew, until in an explosive hour—oh, fifty-one votes against forty-nine—Judas sold his Lord. He came so near *not* doing it, that when he saw what he had done he hanged himself in shame. Ah, Judas, if you had only doubted your doubts enough to wait until Easter, until Pentecost, until Paul came, you would not be the supreme traitor of the centuries. You stood in the presence of divine greatness and you disbelieved.

You see what I am trying to say. Believers can be credulous, but disbelievers too can be gullible fools. Don't join their company! Take a long look at Christ! The world desperately needs him. He is the way and the truth and the life.

Let us apply our theme now to faith in man and his possibilities. Here especially the pessimists are having a field day now.

The kingdom of God on earth—what a dream! What credulity it takes to believe that. On one of our campuses the college paper offered a prize for the best definition of life. Here are some that received honorable mention: "Life is a bad joke which isn't even funny." "Life is a disease for which the only cure is death." "Life is a jail sentence which we get for the crime of being born." My friends, when skepticism, not simply about religion but about human life, is thus carried to its logical conclusion, is it not about time to doubt our doubts?

You see, faith in God concerns something everlastingly so, whether we believe in it or not, but faith in man and his possibilities concerns something which may conceivably become so if we believe in it enough. Only if we have faith in human possibilities can they ever become real. If we all doubt them, they are dished. In this realm faith is creative; doubt is destructive.

Are the skeptics about human hopes the wise men they think they are? Some time since I lectured at the University of Pittsburgh; and I recalled a man named Arthur Lee, who, in 1770, visited the present site of Pittsburgh and in his travel diary wrote this: "The place, I believe, will never be very considerable." There is the skeptic for you, multiplied millions of times in history, blind, blind as bats, to the possibilities which they lacked faith to see. Shakespeare was everlastingly right:

> Our doubts are traitors,
> And make us lose the good we oft might win,
> By fearing to attempt.

This truth which we are trying to make clear becomes most intimate when we apply it to our personal lives. God knows how many here today are burdened with the sense of failure—moral failure, it may be, so that they disbelieve in themselves and doubt that anything worth while can be made of their lives. Look at me, someone is saying, God would have to work a miracle to change me. Well, do you think that kind of miracle is incredible? Listen! I vividly recall the afternoon when I was well started on my radio sermon, when suddenly the man at the controls lifted his arms, and stopped me. "It's all off," he said, "the Japanese are attacking Pearl Harbor." What a day! Who can put into words the outraged thoughts we had about those Japanese bombers? My friends, the pilot who led the attack on Pearl Harbor is in this country now training to be a Christian missionary. He is Captain Mitsuo Fuchida, and he is going back to preach the gospel to his people. Incredible! one would have thought. No! That kind of miracle has made Christian history for nearly two thousand years. And *you* think that *you* cannot be transformed by the renewing of *your* mind. In God's name, doubt your doubts!

I call you to witness that today I have given doubt fair play. I have said in its favor, I think, the best that can be said. But in this tremendous generation we need men and women who have won through doubt to faith—faith in the possibilities of world organization, faith in interracial brotherhood and the abolition of war, faith in the Christian church and its saving gospel, faith in what God can do in them and through them. I want someone here to come over now from skepticism to conviction. As John Masefield sang it:

> Oh yesterday our little troup
>   was ridden through and through,
> Our swaying, tattered pennons fled,
>   a broken, beaten few,

> And all the summer afternoon they
>   hunted us and slew;
> But tomorrow
> By the living God, we'll try the
>   game anew.[1]

That is faith! May we all doubt our doubts until we get it!

[1] "Tomorrow," from *Collected Poems* by John Masefield. Copyright, 1944, by John Masefield. Reprinted by permission of The Macmillan Company.

The Christian Outlook on Life

THERE are many ways in which Christianity can be described —in terms of its organizations, its theologies, its ethical principles—but it can be thought of also more simply as a way of looking at things. This is suggested by a phrase of Paul in his letter to the Galatians, for which Dr. Goodspeed has furnished a new translation. "We were slaves," says Paul; "to material ways of looking at things." The old translation was, "We . . . were in bondage under the elements of the world," but the phrase "elements of the world," which means nothing to us, came from the current philosophy of that day, and Dr. Goodspeed has put Paul's real meaning into our language. Before they became Christians, he said, they had been slaves to material ways of looking at things.

One is struck at once by the applicability of that phrase to much of our modern life. The worship of money; the passionate pursuit of success conceived in terms of things that can be seen; men and women saying, as in Jesus' parable, "Soul, thou hast much goods laid up for many years; take thine ease, eat, drink, be merry"—all this is familiar. Sometimes it is appallingly attractive and constraining. Harriet Beecher Stowe said that New York City was to her an "agreeable delirium." If it could be called that in those old and simple days, what shall we call it now? With its dominance of things visible, measurable, countable, how it does constantly urge upon us all a set of mind that sees life in terms of material values! Yet was there ever more inward, deep-seated dissatisfaction? Do you know anybody who has a material way of looking at things who is really happy?

Those early Christians also lived in a prosperous material civilization. In this regard the Roman Empire was strikingly like our own time. Consider then the genuineness of this suggestion, born directly out of experience, that Christianity involves a changed point of view, a new outlook, an unaccustomed way of seeing things. The importance of this rests back upon a basic principle. All life consists of two elements: first, the facts; second, our way of looking at them.

Here, for example, is a distressing, irritating, physical limitation. That is a fact in how many lives! If, now, a man has allowed it to hurt his temper, ruin his career, spoil his work, how astonished he may be, reading the biography of Immanuel Kant, to discover that there is another way of looking at it! For Immanuel Kant also had a distressing physical limitation, but he lived his life all the same and did his work. What he said was, "The oppression in my chest remained, for its cause lies in the structure of my body, but I have become master of its influence on my thoughts and actions by turning my attention away from this feeling altogether, just as if it did not at all concern me." A man's way of looking at anything makes a profound difference.

Or here is a successful person—an author, let us say, whose books have challenged the attention of the public and whose name is upon every lip. He grows vain. His air, his strut, his condescension all seem to say, I have done it. Upon the other side, what George Eliot said was this: "My predominant feeling is not that I have achieved anything, but that great, great facts have struggled to find a voice through me and have only been able to speak brokenly." One's way of looking at things makes a deep difference.

When one faces a fact like death, which all of us must face, this truth becomes vivid. How appalling death can be, and is, to some! But Charles Kingsley said, "God forgive me if I am wrong, but I look forward to it with an intense and reverent curiosity." The deep divergence between people lies commonly in their ways of looking at things.

Now, Christianity is a way of seeing life, and no other approach to Christianity more quickly reveals its searching, penetrating quality. The word "conversion" has recently been dropping from our religious vocabulary, but it could well come back again, for conversion is a real experience. It comes in varied ways—this inward transformation—sometimes with strong emotion, sometimes as Paul said by the "renewing of the mind." It can be sudden or gradual, like the swift decision of the Prodigal, "I will arise," or like the long road John Wesley traveled before he saw the light in the Moravian meetinghouse. But always involved in genuine conversion is a new way of seeing life.

In making this approach to Christianity's meaning we come directly into the presence of Christ himself and his method of dealing with men. In those first days, when a disciple came within range of Jesus, he was not initially asked to join a church —there was no church; or to subscribe to a formal creed—there was as yet no creed. He was asked to get a new way of seeing things—a new way of looking at the Sabbath, at the Samaritans, at sinners, at children, at God and man. Jesus' word for "repent" meant "change your mind." This kind of conversion is always radical business. Anybody accustomed to dealing with individuals knows that it is comparatively easy to frame a theory that may gain mental assent, or to argue for an organization so that one may say, I will join it. But it is often desperately difficult to get anybody inwardly to change his way of looking at life.

Let us come, then, to practical grips with this matter. Get a new way of looking at money, said Jesus. "Take heed, and keep yourselves from all covetousness: for a man's life consisteth not in the abundance of the things which he possesseth"; "The life is more than the food, and the body than the raiment"; "Ye cannot serve God and mammon"; all of which is as much as to say, that money may be valuable as a means, but beware of its tendency to become an end.

Nobody in his senses would belittle money as a means. It is indispensable. Jesus himself worked in a carpenter's shop for years; he was no sentimentalist far away from the necessary practicalities of ordinary life. But no man can fail to see the tremendous push of money toward the throne, as though it were not means, but end. It is a good thing for us in America now to listen occasionally to what people on the outside say about us. Gandhi, for example, was a great soul. Once he told a group of his fellow Indians that they would understand us Western friends much better if they would remember that no matter what we say in creed or in church, money is our real God. That is distinctly unpleasant. You may even protest that it is not true. But it is partly true. For wherever money piles up, it is so powerful that it tends to drop the garments of servitude which are proper to it, and to crowd up into the throne, not as servant but as tyrant. That is what the Master meant when he said it was hard for a rich man to enter the kingdom of heaven. Wherever riches abound in an individual's or a society's possession, it is difficult business keeping them in their place. As Ralph Waldo Emerson said, "It is hard to carry a full cup."

I am not thinking of this as primarily an economic and socio-logical matter, although a Christian attitude toward money would make radical differences in our economic life. I am thinking of it as a personal and a family matter. One sees families with a Christian tradition and with a real desire to maintain their Christian affiliations who, constantly played upon by the pressure of what Jesus called "mammon," discover their Christian heritage becoming gradually a thin shell within which the real power, the potent force in their households, is a material way of looking at things. In the light of this experience one sees that it is no use trying adequately to define Christianity in terms of creed, ecclesiasticism and what not. That often does not go to the heart of the matter. The heart of the matter is: what is our way of looking at life day in and day out?

The personal climax of all this comes in our training of children. We talk much about religious education. We try to do our best at it in family and church. But no matter what we teach the children consciously and deliberately about religion, their lives are shaped, mastered and controlled by the ways of looking at things, which they catch from the contagion of the family.

Beneath the thin shell of formal religious training how often a material way of looking at things prevails in our homes!— that what fundamentally matters is money and what money buys, that we must keep the pace in our possessions and our social distinctions, that, no matter what it costs, to shine in the light of what we own is basic. How subtle it all is! How penetratingly it works! How gradually a family gets over into it without quite recognizing where they are going until ever and again you see a household wake up, perhaps too late. The children are hard, selfish, worldly; the finer simplicities that alone make family life worth while have been sacrificed; and from of old a voice is saying, "What doth it profit?"

Did someone think at first that to call Christianity a way of looking at things was shallow? Shallow? Is there anything that searches us more deeply? Is there anything much more needed in our personal, family, business life than this kind of conversion that Paul records among the early Christians? "We were slaves," he said, "to material ways of looking at things."

Again genuine Christianity changes a man's outlook not simply on a detail like money but on the universe as a whole. To Christ this universe was not a vast, blind mechanism crashing ruthlessly on, as materialistic philosophy apprehends it. To him it was the creation of a purposeful God, with intelligent meaning and moral intent behind and in it. Just as soon as a Christian makes such a statement someone is ready to charge that he is endeavoring to dodge the facts. But intelligent Christianity does not want to evade facts; it wants to overpass a superficial way of looking at facts. There are all sorts of ways of looking at anything. There lies the ocean. To a chemist it is H_2O plus. To a fisherman it is a means of livelihood. To a lighthouse keeper it is a dwelling place of fogs and storms where ships need guidance. To an internationalist it is a pathway full of increasing intercommunications, whose growing complexity makes a co-operative world ever more needful. To a poet it is "the round ocean, girdled with the sky." It will not do for any one of us to claim that his point of view exhausts the ocean. It does not. Neither will it do for anyone to claim that his point of view exhausts this vast and varied universe. The chemist is right. So is the geologist. So is the astronomer. But when all the physical sciences together have contributed their material ways of looking at the universe, that is not the whole of the universe either.

Who is it that so has apprehended the universe and given us science? The mind. If you say the universe in its infinitesimal aspects is even more marvelous than in its infinite aspects, who discovered it? The mind. All the universe we know, just because we know it, lies within the apprehension of the mind. If there is anything that lies outside the apprehension of our minds, in so far it is not in our universe, so that it will not do for a man to say that the physical approach to life exhausts its meaning. It does not. At least in some sense this universe is a construct of mind. The ultimate fact which science discovers in this law-abiding cosmos is not physical; it is a mathematical formula, and that is mental, if anything is. Einstein called it "cosmic Intelligence."

In a universe where that is true, where all the universe we know exists within the apprehension of our minds, where intelligence finds the universe intelligible and our minds meet Mind, it will not do to say that a merely physical approach to the cosmos exhausts its meaning. That is as much as to say that the Empire State Building is merely or even mainly physical. The Empire State Building is objectified thought. Take out of it the mathematics that are there, the spiritual elements there—planning, purpose, idea—and you have no Empire State Building. The very substance of the Empire State Building, the essential element which makes it cohere, is mental.

A religious philosophy, therefore, does not try to evade the facts. It tries to overpass a superficial way of looking at the facts, for from everlasting to everlasting in every realm, the things which are seen are temporal and the things which are unseen, eternal.

The practical importance of achieving this transformation in outlook in our generation should be obvious. A materialistic point of view about the universe, increasingly shared, results in cynicism, and cynicism is rampant. Listen to this summary of modern disillusionment: "The cosmos is chaos; the chaos is I; and I am my interstitial glands." That is one way of looking at things. Have some of you tried it? Did it really cover the facts? Did you not find that Browning's experience was yours:

> Just when we are safest, there's a sunset-touch,
> A fancy from a flower-bell, some one's death,
> A chorus-ending from Euripides.

Surely, spiritual facts must be spiritually interpreted.

Have you ever tried to see the stained glass in Chartres Cathedral from the outside? That is one way of looking at it. But if a man contents himself with seeing the Chartres windows from the outside he may well be cynical about them; there is no sense in them. But come inside the cathedral and you cannot be cynical. They are beautiful. So some of us were slaves to a material way of looking at the universe; we were trying to stand on the outside and content ourselves with an external physical view. Seen that way the world had no sense at all. And there is a song of victory in the minds of some of us because, while we *were* slaves, we have moved within now and are seeing reality through mind and spirit.

Once more, genuine Christianity will change a man's outlook, not simply with regard to a detail like money or the sum total of everything, the universe, but with regard to that which is closest to us, ourselves, our human adventure on this planet.

To discover the possibilities in human beings is always a mat-

ter of the way we look at them. Take Simon Peter! Put him
before us and the chances are that Simon would have small
likelihood, in our opinion, of amounting to anything. But see
what Jesus did to him! Jesus did have a way of looking at persons. The discovery of possibilities in any realm depends on this.

In 1843 a senator stood up in the chamber of the United
States Senate and, speaking of the hope of some that there might
be a transcontinental railway which would make Oregon a valuable territory, he said, "To talk about constructing a railroad
to the western shore of this continent manifests a wild spirit of
adventure which I never expected to hear broached in the Senate
of the United States." That is one way of looking at things. You
know that type of man well enough to know how stoutly he
would maintain that he was strong on the facts. These idealists,
he would say, blind to the facts, dream of a transcontinental
railroad. But he was not strong on the facts. The idealists were
right.

So, some months ago, I saw a moral failure, a downright
moral failure, so thoroughgoing that he stood in imminent peril
of the law and, so far as visible facts were concerned, there was
no more chance that he could ever be anything except a failure
than there was, in the senator's mind, a possibility of a transcontinental railroad. Today, however, that man is distinctly not
a failure. In these last few months he has staged one of the most
splendid moral recoveries it has ever been my privilege to see,
and the secret of it all was getting over to him Christ's way of
looking at life.

Always the possibilities of human life depend not simply on
what men who have nothing more than eyes call facts, but on
the way we look at them. What is it that keeps a peaceful border
line between the United States and Canada? That friendly

boundary is guarded by the strongest thing in the world, a mental attitude. And if we could win a sufficient number of people to a genuine Christian way of seeing life, every border line on earth would be as safe.

How is it, then, with us? Tomorrow we are going back into that old world. The facts will be pretty much what they were. But our lives do not need to be what they were. We have only a limited control over facts, but we have a large control over our ways of seeing them. And when a man gets a new way of seeing he has a new life. From everlasting to everlasting that thing is true which long ago the seer said; to be carnally minded—physically, materially minded—is death; but to be spiritually minded is life and peace.

Life's Forced Decisions

R ELIGIOUS confusion and uncertainty are nothing new. We
have just sung "Lead, Kindly Light"—a hymn born out of
the travail of a soul distracted over his religion. Nevertheless, our
new science, forcing the radical reconstruction of our thought,
has accentuated our modern bewilderment. Religious opinions
are painfully upset. Multitudes of people do not know what
they think. The winds of doctrine are gusty and variable. There
have been times of comparatively unanimous opinion in religion
with a settled, strong and single wind that blew one way, but
not now. In this congregation there must be many of us who
even when faced with basic matters of religious faith—God,
Christ, the Bible, prayer or immortality—often ask ourselves in
our own secret thinking what our opinion is. Not at all because
I desire to avoid that issue, but to come at it by a fresh approach,
I raise with you another question. James, the Lord's brother—
in a different setting, to be sure—asked that question in the
fourth chapter of his letter and the fourteenth verse: "What is
your life?" Not now, What is your opinion about this religious
matter or that? but "What is your life?"

A clear contrast confronts us between the question that so
commonly bewilders us in matters of religion, What is our opinion? and this question that James asks, What is our life? We can
postpone answering the question about our opinion. What is our

opinion about God? We may not be able to answer that. We
may pick it up, dally with it, try this idea for an answer and
then that, make up our minds that it is desperately difficult to
find an answer, and lay the whole question down finally unde-
cided.

> Myself when young did eagerly frequent
> Doctor and Saint, and heard great argument
> About it and about: but evermore
> Came out by the same door where in I went.

That is a familiar experience, and the result is agnosticism—
not dogmatic atheism but reverent agnosticism. Many cannot
make up their minds. They find that every argument has a
counterargument; often the opposing considerations seem like
Tweedledee and Tweedledum; if you ask them what they think
about God, the soul and immortality, they say they do not know.
While, however, we can thus avoid answering the question,
What is our opinion? we cannot avoid answering the question,
What is our life? For here is a fact so momentous that no single
sermon can sum up its significance, that, while we can avoid
making up our minds, we cannot avoid making up our lives. The
older a man grows, the more that towering fact impresses him.
We can hold our opinions in suspense, but we cannot hold our
living in suspense. We live one way or the other.

Shall you go to college, for example, or shall you go directly
from high school into business? That is a debatable question.
There may be opposing considerations about which with open
and unprejudiced mind you would better think. You may not
be able to make up your mind. But you will have to make up
your life. For the relentless march of living does not stop for any
inconclusiveness in your debate, and soon or late, at the fork

of the road, willy-nilly, you will go one way or the other, either to college or not to college. If opinion does not force decision, life will.

Or consider the debate between the protagonists of monogamous marriage on the one side, and temporary liaisons and promiscuity on the other. You may face with suspended judgment the opposing considerations. You may not be able to make up your mind. But you do have to make up your life. One way or the other you will live, either going back to the polygamous instinct, or else being true to that finest thing that has evolved in the history of family relationships, the instinct of monogamy.

To be sure, there are areas of life where our opinions do not affect our living and hence where our living does not force decision about our opinions. As to which of the various theories concerning the atmosphere on Mars is true I do not know. One does not have to know. One does not even have to guess. One does not have to make up his mind about that because one does not have to make up his life about that. That is not a forced decision.

But most of the troublesome questions that seriously perplex us are forced decisions. You have to make up your life one way or the other. They remind one of being in a rowboat, going down a powerful river and debating whether or not to stop at a given point. There may be opposing considerations that an open and unprejudiced mind ought to face. Continue, then, your debate as to whether or not you will stop. But in the meantime the river has not waited the conclusion of your argument and sooner or later, if your debate has not decided the question, the river conclusively will have settled it. You will not have stopped. How much like life that is you know well.

This morning our proposition is that religion is a forced decision. Of course, many details of religion are not that. As to whether you will be a Baptist or an Episcopalian is not a forced decision. You do not need to make up your mind about such propositions because you do not need to make up your life about them. But intimate, vital, personal religion, the total reaction of a personality to the whole meaning of life—that is a forced issue. Whether or not this universe is aimless or whether there is purpose at the heart of it; whether it all came from the fortuitous self-arrangement of atoms or whether our lives and labors are sustained by a Being, most like intelligence and goodwill when at their best they rise in us; whether Christ is a revelation of something deep at the heart of Reality or a psychological spark struck off from physical collisions; and whether the end of it all is a coffin and an ash heap or an open sepulcher and a hope— you have to live one way or the other.

Remember George Bernard Shaw's remark: "What a man believes may be ascertained not from his creed, but from the assumptions on which he habitually acts." By no possibility can anybody avoid assumptions on which he habitually acts. Watch your own life. Watch any other man's life. Forty years old, fifty years old, sixty years old—you will see how ever more clearly appear those underlying and directive assumptions on which he habitually acts. He may never have said to himself that he had made up his mind. He may never have thought he had achieved a definite opinion. But he could not help making up his life. That was a forced issue.

For one thing, what is your life with reference to your faith in God? In one sense God is not a matter of faith at all, but a matter of fact. We deal here obviously with creative Power. That is as clear as the electricity that drives our machines and lights our houses. Creative Power is behind this universe, and through it, producing everything that is and driving it. That is fact. Moreover, not by faith but by factual experience we do know some important things about this Power. It is law-abiding; it never slips its leash. It is beautifying; it makes the sunsets and the colors of a peacock's tail, and in the dark depths of the sea, where no eye looks, it creates small crustaceans whose structure is as balanced and beautiful as the oriel window of a Gothic cathedral. Strange Power! It makes volcanoes and Easter lilies; it makes a jewel of purest ray serene and tornadoes and earthquakes; it creates the crocodile and hippopotamus and the babe at Mary's breast. Strange Power! It rises into personality, into minds that range the universe and grasp its laws, into characters that are incandescent with beauty, truth and goodness, holding high faith about God and destiny, into social progress that swings up the spiral from some ancient stone age and with Walt Whitman sings of "Health, peace, salvation universal."

These things that we have just described are not matters of faith; they are matters of fact. This creative Power is actually here. These consequences of its operation we do see, so that in that sense God is not so much something that we believe in as observe.

But when we come to interpret that creative Power, then opinions differ. That creative Power might be merely physical. Atoms and electrons swishing around in an empty void might fortuitously have arranged themselves into all that is. You have seen a giant printing press into which at one end goes raw paper, and from which at the other end comes the finished product, marked all over with the signs of thought, idea, ideal, aspiration, purpose. An amazing thing—a machine did that. So, the universe might be a machine—strange that it made itself!—into which raw matter enters at one end and from the other automatically comes humanity with its arts, its sciences, its religion. That might be.

To be sure, when one uses any symbol, drawn from human experience, as a description of God, one must do it with humility—it is bound to be partial and inadequate. Thus a little child, beginning the study of geography, may think of Italy as like a boot. So it is—like a boot, thrust out into the Mediterranean—but how little that says of all that should be said about Italy! Far more inadequate than that are all our symbolic names for God. Nevertheless, behind our partial symbols, in terms of which we think of God, there still may be God, and as electricity, which suffuses the universe, may illumine our homes, so the Eternal Spirit may become light and life and power in our lives.

Our proposition today is that we cannot be altogether neutral on that point. If I ask you what your opinion is you may say you have not made up your mind, but what is your life? You are living one way or the other. You young people here this morning may not believe that at first. You may suppose that on a matter like faith in God you can be quite neutral in your living. But you cannot.

Love comes into your life radiant and beautiful, and you do inevitably tend to take one attitude or the other, either that it is a revelation of something deep at the heart of Reality or else a fortuitous by-product of a physical process. Work comes into your life, sometimes very hard, disappointing, onerous, costing sacrifice, and you do inevitably tend to take one attitude or the other, either that it is small use trying to do anything for these blundering, animal automata that we call men, or else that our Father works hitherto and we work, and that all faithful labor begun, continued and ended in him will not fail of its final fruits. Trouble comes into your life, devastating, crushing, and you do inevitably tend to take one attitude or the other, either, as one put it, that life is "a nightmare between two nothings" or else, as Browning said, that life, for all its trouble, is

> . . . just a stuff
> To try the soul's strength, educe the man.

Your life does get made up one way or the other.

Anatole France, the French littérateur, ought to have been happy. What did he lack to make a man happy? Creative gifts, large achievement, the adulation of countless friends, plenty of material resources—why should he not have been happy? Listen to him: "There is not in all the universe a creature more unhappy than I. People think me happy. I have never been happy for one day, not for a single hour." He was an utter skeptic about any spiritual significance in life, and life does get made up one way or the other.

Or William Wilberforce—should he not have been unhappy? After a long life fighting for the abolition of the British slave trade, at seventy-one years of age he lost his fortune. Accustomed to wealth and comfort, he had to leave his favorite residence at threescore years and ten and seek a home with his married sons. Should he not, too, have been unhappy? Yet two days after he learned the full extent of his losses we read this in his diary: "A solitary walk with the psalmist—evening quiet." You see, life gets made up one way or the other.

I am not trying to avoid the merely intellectual arguments about belief in God. I would agree on intellectual grounds alone with one of our leading American philosophers that, of all systems of magic ever offered to the credulity of man, there never was a system of magic so incredible as the proposition that a number of physical particles fortuitously moving in an empty void could arrange themselves into planets, sunsets, mothers, music, art, science, poetry, Christ. Materialism is not thinking through philosophy. Materialism is running away from philosophy to believe in magic.

This morning, however, we are getting at the question from another approach. The decision between God and no-God, between an aimless and a purposeful universe, is not forced by your opinion but by your life. Do you say this morning that you are an agnostic, that you are neutral? What is your life? It is being made up one way or the other.

Again, what is your life with reference to faith in man? For not only is God a matter both of fact and of faith; man is also. Here are all the facts about man, very obvious to most of us, but what do you make of them? How do you interpret them? Is man, for example, a merely physical machine with some interesting mental and spiritual by-products?

To be sure, that idea presents serious difficulties. We human beings are not only driven from behind but are lured by ideals ahead of us, enticed by chosen goals and purposes. We even cry with Tennyson,

> . . . Ah for a man to arise in me,
> That the man I am may cease to be!

Imagine a machine doing that! And we human beings repent—sometimes with heartbreaking remorse—for wrongs done, and penitently seek pardon and make restitution. No machine ever did that. And we human beings look up to Something above us, however we may describe the values we reverence; we sometimes even "love the highest when we see it," and give ourselves to it with selfless dedication. Picture a machine doing that!

When, then, our materialistic friends insist that we human beings are mere machines, while we grant that it is quite obvious that there is a mechanistic aspect to us all, one wonders what simpletons they think us to be that we should be so frightened and hoodwinked by a word. At least they must acknowledge that we are machines that think, love, distinguish between right and wrong, repent, follow ideals, sacrifice for one another, believe in God, hope for immortality, and construct philosophies to explain the universe. Queer machines! Nevertheless, we might be, I suppose, some kind of physicochemical product. Or it might be, on the other hand, that the deeper truth lies in the ancient faith that "we are children of God: and if children, then heirs; heirs of God, and joint-heirs with Christ."

This morning we are saying that we cannot be neutral on that question. If I should ask you what your opinion is you might say you have no opinion, but we are asking a deeper question today: What is your life? For, soon or late, assumptions do appear in your life with reference to human value and destiny, on which you habitually act.

Put over against each other two extreme views of this question—the estimate of man that Jesus had, when he died for man because he thought man was worth dying for, and on the other side H. L. Mencken's estimate. Says Mr. Mencken: "The cosmos is a gigantic fly-wheel making 10,000 revolutions a minute." "Man is a sick fly taking a dizzy ride on it." "The basic fact about human existence is not that it is a tragedy, but it is a bore. It is not so much a war as an endless standing in line. The objection to it is not that it is predominantly painful, but that it is lacking in sense." And when it comes to anything like politics he calls it "a combat between jackals and jackasses." You see, this business of thinking about man is not simply a question of theory, it is a question of life. At twenty years of age you may not be aware of the assumptions on which habitually you act. At forty years of age your friends will be aware of them. At fifty years of age you will be singularly lacking in introspection if the assumptions on the basis of which you habitually act have not now become conscious. At sixty years of age everybody, yourself included, will know what these assumptions are. You can no more escape that than water can stay poised on the edge of the ridge and resist the importunity of gravitation. On the one side you will have been pulled by the gravitation of strong faith toward the conclusion that human beings have endless possibilities worth working for, or down the other side you will have been pulled by the gravitation of cynicism toward the conclusion that human life, fundamentally, is not worth living.

Is there someone here today who has thought himself neutral on this question? You are fooling yourself about your neutrality. What is your life?

Once more, this same truth holds about faith in the future, about hope and hopelessness. It may be that death ends all, that this generation is a bonfire to warm the hands of the next generation and that that generation will be another bonfire to warm the hands of the next, and that in the end this whole human conflagration on the planet will burn itself out and end in an ash heap. That might be. Or it might be that, the Creative Power at the heart of all things being spiritual, the creative process cannot end in an ash heap, that every Calvary will have its Easter day and every winter its spring, that this corruptible must put on incorruption and this mortal put on immortality, and what eye hath not seen nor ear heard is laid up as a consummation for the spiritual life that upon this earth has had so promising a start. That might be true.

As between these two possibilities, we cannot get a Q.E.D. answer. We cannot work the argument out to absolute finality. And so, because it is so difficult to get an assured answer, people think that they will reserve their opinions and not make up their minds. But what is your life? For, my friends, hope and hopelessness are not simply theories. They are ways of living. Consider Omar Khayyám:

> Oh threats of Hell and Hopes of Paradise!
> One thing at least is certain—*This* Life flies:
> One thing is certain and the rest is Lies;
> The flower that once has blown for ever dies.

That is a way of living.

A famous scientific investigator once said to a friend of mine that the greatest tragedy that ever had happened in this universe was the evolution of consciousness. He lived, that is, in a universe so dark and damnable that the greatest tragedy that ever happened was that human beings should develop consciousness to know how dark and damnable it is! Such hopelessness, my friends, is a way of living.

It may be that there are some here this morning whose life is better than their creed. If we should ask them whether they believe in God, the soul and immortality, they would say, No, we do not. But they live as though they did. We all know people whose life is better than their creed.

There probably are folk here whose life is worse than their creed. How many of us in a resounding declaration would say that of course we believe in God, in man as God's child, and in immortality as man's goal. Do we really? *What is our life?*

And there surely would be some here who would say that they do not know, that they have tried to make up their mind and could not. They might even say emphatically that they have stopped trying to answer such unanswerable questions. Have you really? *What is your life?* It is being made up one way or the other. Neutrality is a figment of the imagination on any basic issue of life. To live as though this were a godless, purposeless universe, as though human life were a combat between jackals and jackasses, a combat whose end is to be a coffin and an ash heap, that is hell on earth. And to live as though God were the kind of being whom Christ revealed, as though man, God's child, had boundless possibilities worth working for, and as though in the end

> All we have willed or hoped or dreamed of good
>   shall exist;
> Not its semblance, but itself,

that is heaven on earth. What is your life?

Despise Ye the Church of God?

WE are confronting ourselves this morning with the question: Despise ye the church of God? Modern as it sounds, as though it had for its background contemporary censures of the church, it was, as a matter of fact, asked long ago by Paul in the eleventh chapter of his first letter to the Corinthians. Even then people were showing despite to the church and manifesting by deed and word how little they respected it. Changed though the circumstances are from the day when Paul's question rose, it still is pertinent and multitudes of our contemporaries would return to it a resounding affirmative. They do despise the church. They might even, like Swinburne, the poet, express admiration for the Nazarene while they condemn his "leprous bride," the church.

In the face of this censure, commonly visited upon the churches, a sensitive churchman's first instinct is to find some method of rebuttal. He wants to answer back. To be sure, he might say, plenty of people contemn the church but that is only camouflage for their rejection of the life and character for which the church is standing. They blame the outward institution whereas the fact is they will not accept the quality of faith and life for which the institution stands. Like a man complaining about a volume of Shakespeare that the print is too fine or the page is too small or the volume too heavy, when all the while he does not want to read Shakespeare at all but the last detective story, so people blame the outward church when they have no use for the thing which the church represents.

Undoubtedly that kind of evasion does exist in many assailants of the church; yet that is no adequate dealing with our problem. There are real reasons on account of which serious people censure the church.

Or, again, a sensitive churchman might say, all these faults for which the churches are condemned are but the common and familiar foibles of humanity. You find them in every organization man builds. Why should we be peculiarly attacked for these common failures of mankind? They accuse us of sectarianism. Look, then, at medicine. One might suppose that in dealing with the body, which the eye can see and the hands handle, we could achieve complete agreement of opinion, but what with allopathy, homeopathy, osteopathy, chiropractic, and how many more schools of healing who can say, it is plain that sectarianism afflicts medicine as well as religion. So the sensitive churchman, tired of being accused of common human faults, turns on his assailants and says, You're another!

That is true, and yet it is not an adequate handling of the situation. It would be a pity if in building an institution to represent Jesus Christ we could say only that we are no worse than others. We should not content ourselves with easy rebuttals. The churches deserve to be censured. The churches need reformation. There are just reasons for deep and anxious concern about them, and the first prerequisite for their reorganization is that we of the churches should be discontented with them, deeply, persistently, loyally discontented with them.

I am thinking, for example, of some young man here who

may be considering the Christian ministry. He feels at times a flame within, as though the day might come when he could speak some burning words that might set other men afire. And yet he says, Look at the churches! I do not agree with a single one of them. I adore Christ and would gladly spend my life making his principles regnant in the individual characters and the social relationships of men, but these churches! Their dividing lines do not correspond with a single real interest in modern life. Their creeds and rituals, rigidly insisted on for membership and ordination, are like Procrustean beds on which the modern mind, when laid, is impossibly stretched out or incontinently sawed off. I believe in Christ, but these churches!

To which I answer, Young man, on the basis of your own statement, I beg of you, come into the Christian ministry. You are precisely the kind of man most needed. A young man who agrees with any single church or with all of them together is thereby disqualified for the largest effectiveness in the ministry. We need no more complacent clergymen.

Lately I visited a southern community—twelve hundred inhabitants, nine churches. Content with that? Only this last week I had a letter from a student who lately studied on this hill telling of a western community grossly overchurched, the little sects cut off from one another by rigid creeds and practices, no serious work being done by any of them for children and youth, no touch from all of them together on young people, their thinking and their playing, six days a week. Content with that?

Keshab Chandar Sen, one of the religious leaders of India, said, "I do believe, and I must candidly say, that no Christian sect puts forth the genuine and full Christ as he was and as he is, but, in some cases, a mutilated, disfigured Christ, and, what is more shameful, in many cases, a counterfeit Christ." Content with the situation which causes thoughtful Indians to say that? No, my friend, if you are going into the Christian ministry, go, not because you are contented with the ecclesiastical status quo but because you hear the hour strike for another reformation of the church of Christ.

Nevertheless, while the first prerequisite of better days in organized religion is that we of the churches should be deeply and loyally discontented, the second is close alongside: that we have faith in the church.

Like the deep and quiet sea beneath the tossing waves, so beneath our censures must be a steadfast faith in the church of Christ. He who scorns the church is useless to it. Despise *ye* the church of God?

In the first place, if we are to return a hearty negative to that question it will be because we do believe in what churches at their best are trying to say. We are tempted in this country to be critical also of our courts of law. The administration of criminal justice in this nation is a public disgrace, President Taft once said. Yet if there should arise a revolutionary movement that cried, Down with the courts! we would all rally to their support. For, while it is true that the administration of justice needs reformation, it is also true that what the law courts at their best are trying to say must be said. They may stammer at it; nevertheless the thing which the courts at their best are trying to say must be said: namely, that justice should be administered in orderly fashion. Now, if someone should say, I believe in justice but not in the courts, we would resent that evasion. To believe in justice in the abstract, where there are no practical difficulties, but evade the organization of justice in courts where all the real difficulties lie, is sheer folly. It always is messy, harassing, compromising, difficult business to organize any high ideal into a working institution, but it is sheer hypocrisy to pretend to believe in the high ideal and run away from the endeavor to make it practically work. Therefore, despite their clear insight into the need of legal reformation, serious citizens stand by the courts because they believe what the courts at their best are trying to say.

So, I, for one, stand by the church. I returned once from a visit to the Orient. I had been in parts of the world where there are no Christian churches and never have been and against that background every little Christian meetinghouse, seen from the car window as we crossed this continent, seemed to be speaking, and one kept listening to what those churches at their best were trying to say. Someone protests that they stutter. Yes, they do. Some of them stutter badly; yet, for all their stuttering, consider what at their best they are trying to say: No civilization ever can survive, no matter how high it pile material means for living, if it neglects the spiritual ends of life. At their best they are trying to say that. What shall it profit a man, or a city, or a nation, to gain the whole world and lose the soul? At their best they are trying to say that.

How mysterious is this human pilgrimage, born out of darkness, weaving its tangled way for a few years amid joy and sorrow here, falling at last on the final mystery of death!

> Yet, in the maddening maze of things,
>   And tossed by storm and flood,
> To one fixed trust my spirit clings;
>   I know that God is good!

They are trying to say that.

"Pure religion and undefiled before our God and Father is

this, to visit the fatherless and widows in their affliction, and to keep onself unspotted from the world." "If any man hath not the Spirit of Christ, he is none of his." "Not every one that saith unto me, Lord, Lord, shall enter into the kingdom of heaven; but he that doeth the will of my Father." At their best they are trying to say that.

Some time ago I stood beside an open grave where two lovers laid the body of their little child. I had married them, in the name of the church sealing the pledges of their love, and now in the hour of their grief I stood beside them, in the name of the church sealing their sorrow with its message of hope. The churches are trying to say that.

The fisherfolk of Brittany have a legend that off their coast, deep sunken in the sea, is the ideal community of Atlantis and that sometimes, when the nights are clear and the winds are quiet, if a man's heart is right, he can hear the pealing of the bells. So is the soul of man, with sacred things deep hidden in him that the storms of this world cause us to forget. But, sometimes, quieted in worship, a man can hear the pealing of his bells. And the church is trying to say that.

Indeed, today my personal recollections go far off from this scene of Gothic grandeur to a little brick meetinghouse in the Chautauqua hills. It was a poor place when I was a boy; it is a poor place yet. It never was rich and prosperous; it always was one of the smallest churches in town. Moreover, it preached an old theology that I cannot believe, and stood for denominational peculiarities in which I am utterly uninterested now. But one morning, in that church—ah, my soul, remember!—I, as a boy, caught a glimpse of the vision glorious. Every man has shrines of pilgrimage. That is one of the chief of mine, that little brick meetinghouse in the Chautauqua hills, for there I, as a boy, moved up from this faulty church visible into the church invisible and eternal.

Have you never seen a chromo of the Sistine Madonna? What a poor representation! you say. Yes, but the Sistine Madonna itself is so beautiful that even a chromo catches something of its dignity. You say these churches are imperfect. They are very imperfect, but they are the imperfect representations of something without which humanity cannot live. Despise ye the church of God?

In the second place, if a man is to return a hearty negative to that question, it will be because he sees that even these imperfect, visible churches are a long way from dead. They are going concerns. We had better not despise the church. Within its ample borders now are about one-third the population of the globe. These churches wield a tremendous influence for good or evil over multitudes of men. When they are stupid, backward-looking, unintelligent, superstitious, the effect is terrific. When they are intelligent, forward-looking, enlightened, ethically-minded, recapturing the essential message of the Master and applying it courageously to modern life, the consequences are inestimably beneficial. The noblest achievements in this nation are impossible without the right kind of churches. What happens to the Christian church in these next years is one of the most crucial problems of our civilization. Whatever else our attitude is we would better not despise the church.

But someone says, these sectarian denominations! I agree. They are lamentable. The differences between them no more appertain to modern life than the boundaries of ancient Indian tribes do to the United Nations, and yet even here there is

something oft forgotten which may well be said. You who plead
for the union of Christendom, Christendom once was united.
Once there was only one church. Once the communion of saints
was a chain gang at lock step with one long whip cracking down
the line to prevent any man's deviating from that one control,
and in those days our fathers broke loose and struck out for air
to breathe. Now forward-looking and progressive men are trying
to bring the churches together; then intelligent and progressive
men were working against a tyrannical unity in the interest of a
diversity that would give them liberty. Say what you will about
the denominations, in those days when Martin Luther nailed
his Theses to the doors at Wittenberg and dared the ancient
church, or when John Calvin started an intellectual bonfire in
Geneva that lightened Europe, or when John Knox in Edin-
burgh was "lyk to ding the pulpit in blads" pleading for the
principles of the Reformation that split Christendom, or when
John Wesley went out from a Moravian prayer meeting in London to preach a gospel that set the English-speaking race on fire
although he did divide the English Establishment, or when, as
the biographer of John Milton says about the Baptists, "It was,
in short, from their little dingy meetinghouse, somewhere in Old
London, that there flashed out, first in England, the absolute
doctrine of Religious Liberty"—in those days, strong, courageous
men were working for denominations and some of the finest
things in modern spiritual life have come from those who, in the
day when denominations were needed, dared create them.

If now, like all good things, these sects once useful have out-
grown their usefulness and should be overpassed to something
better, we need not be discouraged. See how far we have gone
already on that road!

Once the churches persecuted each other with gibbet and

stake. Then out of the age of persecution they moved into the age of controversy, concerning which another sang:

> And most of all thank God for this:
> The war and waste of clashing creeds
> Now end in words and not in deeds,
> And no one suffers loss or bleeds
> For thoughts which men call heresies.

Then, out of the age of controversy they moved into the age of toleration, where they endured one another, looked askance at one another, were suspicious of one another. Now, from the age of toleration they have moved out into the age of co-operation, seeing that, as in a watch, some wheels go one way and some another, yet all conspire to make the hands go round, so it may be with the churches. Do you think we are going to stop there? From persecution to controversy, from controversy to toleration, from toleration to co-operation, from co-operation to unity—so moves the church of Christ.

Once more, if we are to return a resounding negative to this question, it will be because we see how much we personally need the church. I can well understand those who say they do not need it. If it will be a source of good courage to some young person here, let me say that there was a time in my college life when forty wild horses could hardly drag me inside the church, when I was confident that I could be as good a Christian as I needed without the church and, like Kipling's cat, walked by my "wild lone." But I should suppose that a man who seriously wants to live the Christian life would outgrow that.

In a day when so many of our social groupings drag us down by the pull of their mob-mindedness, who does not need a social grouping that levels him up, where once in a while at least he meets with his fellows on the basis of our noblest faiths and our finest aspirations? In the summertime have you never seen a twig snap out of a bonfire and burn alone? For a while it burns in reminiscence of the fire it came from and then goes out, for fire comes from fellowship.

Nevertheless, I can understand a man saying, But I am getting on very well without the church. To which I answer, Getting on without the church? Not in America. If you want really to get on without the church you will have to go a long way from here, perchance to the highlands of Tibet. For in this country you are surrounded on every side by traditions that came out of the church, by families whose roots are in the church, by ideas and ideals that were born from the church, and by men and women who believe in the church. In the United States you cannot live without the church.

A mandarin's daughter from China came to the United States years ago to study in one of our women's colleges, and specialized in English literature. One day she went to her professor and said, "I am puzzled. Every time I read a great classic of the English speech I find ideas and ideals that seem to be common property and are different from anything in my own land. There must be a reason. What is the source?" And the professor said, "Do you know the Bible?" "No," she replied, "I never read it." "Well," he answered, "if you are going to understand English literature you will have to know the Bible." To be sure! Take out of English literature what got there directly or indirectly from the Scriptures and what you will have left is like a bombed town.

When a man, therefore, in a community like this, says he is living without the church, it is not impressive. I will tell you what it would mean to live without the church. Let the church die. Let generation after generation rise that never knew it. Let Jesus become a myth, the message of the Bible forgotten, faith in God nebulous, worship finished, no more sacred music now, only secular; no more religious education of the children now, only secular; a literature from which have been deleted the ideas and ideals that have their rootage in religious heritage—then you could live without the church. Do you wish to try?

And if you must confess that in that real sense you do not desire to live without the church, may I not invite some of you to come into closer co-operation with the Christian fellowship? For, mark it! my friends, a full Christianity involves fellowship. There are great musical compositions which no artist, however fine, can play alone. No matter how well that first violinist can play, he cannot interpret them alone. It takes an orchestra—the oboes and violas and violins, the flutes and drums and horns—to interpret such great compositions. And Christianity is great. No soloist alone can render it. Ah, you solitary piccolo, trying to render the Overture to *Tannhäuser!* It cannot be done. But you might help. Even if nobody noticed you, you might help—in the orchestra.

The Danger of Going to Church

MINISTERS commonly talk about churchgoing, but what they usually say about it is that we *ought* to go to church; and they quote the Bible to show that it is a duty. Today I confront myself and you with something else in the Bible about churchgoing which troubles me—its scathing disapproval of churchgoers. To be sure, the Bible repeatedly calls us to worship; tells us that Jesus himself went to the synagogue, as his custom was, on the sabbath day; and in the words of the apostle warns us: "Forsake not the assembling of yourselves together, as the custom of some is!"

There is, however, another aspect of the Bible's message. Read that first chapter of Isaiah, where in the Temple, crowded with worshipers, the prophet hears God indignantly saying to the throng: "Who hath required this at your hand, to trample my courts?" So *that* is what churchgoing can degenerate into— temple trampling!

Jesus himself pictured a Pharisee going up to the Temple to pray. That is a pious practice which we have had urged on us from our youth up. But, says Jesus, that man stood in the Temple and prayed with himself, saying, "Lord, I thank Thee, that I am not as the rest of men." One of the most sarcastic things Jesus ever said about anybody was about people who, as he put it, "love to stand and pray in the synagogues." Especially, recall that sabbath when Jesus spoke to the crowded sanctuary in Nazareth about interracial goodwill, about God's grace caring for Syrians and Sidonians just as much as for Jews. All the churchgoers that day, we read, "rose up, and cast him forth out of the city." You see what I am getting at. According to the Bible, some of God's worst trouble has been with churchgoers.

In this nation now church membership has reached an all-time high and, while attendance doubtless varies in different localities—and, as another put it, the easiest way to increase a congregation is to estimate it—it is not untypical that recently in the Middle West I talked with a minister who has three identical services every Sunday morning to accommodate the people. Many Christians are encouraged by these crowded churches. So am I. But then comes that second thought. Why are all these people coming to church? What are they seeking, and what are they really getting out of it?

Let us take it for granted that many of us here know what going to church at its best can mean—inward reinforcement, clear vision of duty, restored faith and courage, as though in a smog the northwest wind blew, the sun shone again, and the horizons cleared. We come in faltering; we go out "strengthened with might by his Spirit in the inner man." We find in the church's worship interior illumination and resource, in the light and strength of which we go out, our better selves on top again, to build lovelier homes and to work for a more Christian world for children to be born in. That is churchgoing at its best.

One reason, I suspect, why Isaiah heard God condemning the temple-tramplers was that once he himself, in the Temple, had had an experience which changed his whole life. He knew what going to the Temple could mean. He saw God there, high and lifted up, and heard a divine voice saying to him, "Whom shall

I send, and who will go for us?" and Isaiah answered, "Here am I; send me." That experience made history. That was church-going on the grand scale.

But come down to earth now and face more familiar kinds of churchgoers: formal, conventional observers of decent fashion on Sunday morning; fans of popular preachers, as of movie stars; people who think that church attendance is a useful family practice, and not unhelpful to one's reputation; sectarian minds, coming from church with all their bigotries sharpened and con-firmed; mere peace-of-mind seekers, lulled by music and prayer into easygoing tranquillity, using worship, as another put it, "as a sort of glorified aspirin tablet"; and even hypocrites, covering unworthy lives under the outward show of religious respectabil-ity—all sorts of churchgoers.

We had better face this fact, as the Bible does. And do not, I beg of you, think of me as a preacher hurling accusations at you. After a minister has retired, as I have, he begins spending his Sunday mornings in the pew. He joins the ranks of the churchgoers. I am one of you. I am asking myself: What kind of churchgoer am I?

To begin with, it is easy to see how church attendance can become trivial and futile. Of all the millions who attend church in this country, for example, how many are merely spectators? So they go to a football game, but they do not themselves play ball; they watch others play. So they go to the theater, but do not themselves act; they watch others act. So they come to church and watch the ministers and the choir worship in the chancel, and comment on how well or ill they do it. They are spectators, not participants. Nothing vital, renewing, transform-ing, happens inside them. What a pity!

Or think of all the people to whom church attendance is only a pious formality. One of religion's most dangerous aspects is that it makes sacred everything it touches, so that all sorts of externals can become invested with hallowed meaning, until outwardly to observe them is mistaken for genuine religion. Nowhere is this substitution of ritual observance for vitality more obvious than in some churchgoers.

> They do it every Sunday,
> They'll be all right on Monday.
> It's just a little habit
>   they've acquired.

I almost hesitate to quote what some of our wisest minds have said about the possible meaning of coming to church. Said Professor Wieman of the University of Chicago about worship: "There is no other form of human endeavor by which so much can be accomplished." Said President Eliot of Harvard, thinking of inspiring Sundays in the chapel: "Prayer is the greatest achievement of the human soul." James Russell Lowell went to church once and came out singing:

> This life were brutish did we not sometimes
> Have intimation clear of wider scope,
> Hints of occasion infinite, to keep
> The soul alert with noble discontent
> And onward yearnings of unstilled desire;
> Fruitless, except we now and then divined
> A mystery of Purpose, gleaming through
> The secular confusions of the world.

We cannot brush such men off as pious fools. They are talking about something real. Here in this church today, with the great tradition of the Christian heritage around us, with Christ's way of life exalted above the sordid level of our vulgar world, with

God calling us to lift up our eyes unto the hills from whence cometh our help, we are all within reach of wealth for our souls, which can make us resourceful, secure, confident, dedicated, strong. Don't miss it! Don't give God occasion to say to anyone here: "Who hath required this at your hand, to trample my courts?"

Now let us come to grips with two vital aspects of church-going which we are all in danger of missing.

First, coming to church can issue in renewed, sustained, dedicated personal character. It can make an ethical difference in our daily living. We sing the praises of Sir Wilfred Grenfell. What a man! But many do not know where that strong, devoted life started. Wilfred Grenfell went to church—that's where it started. Dwight L. Moody conducted the service, and it could not have been a very dignified affair, for Moody asked one of the ministers to lead in prayer, and he did—he prayed and prayed, on and on, until at last Moody rose and said: "While the brother is finishing his prayer, let us sing hymn 161!" No! It was no glorious architecture in Moody's tabernacle nor any esthetic impressiveness in the service that did the business in Grenfell. Grenfell himself really worshiped God that day, so that finding his worse self confronted by his better self, and his better self confronted by Christ who is better yet, he went out, a transformed, redirected character to make his life count for the Kingdom. That is going to the church at its best.

Today there is a popular movement afoot in our churches which loses sight of this deep ethical meaning in public worship. I refer to the obsession of many of our new churchgoers with peace of mind and nothing else. To be sure, peace of mind is a basic spiritual need, and in this upset generation many of these

new churchgoers are rightly seeking in Christian faith the cure
of their anxieties and fears. The trouble is that to some of these
new churchgoers peace of mind becomes an end in itself. The
church to them is simply a place of escape, an island of safety, a
pillow to lie down on, an ivory tower. All they want of it is inner
tranquillity—period! We sing, "Like a mighty army moves the
Church of God." Well, an army has hospitals and rehabilita-
tion centers, where shocked and battered soldiers are put to
rights again, but the end in view is to return them to the fray.
So the church should minister to sick souls, helping them to find
in religious faith a peace-giving antidote for their disheveled
worries. But tranquillity alone does not make a Christian. Too
many churchgoers use religion as a sedative. We blame Lenin
for calling religion "the opiate of the people," but it was a Christian minister, Charles Kingsley, who said *that* before Lenin did.
Kingsley was manfully fighting for some desperately needed social reforms in England, and he saw too many churchgoers who,
far from being aroused by the clarion call to seek the Kingdom
of God, were using the church as an opiate. Friends, if Christ
were in this pulpit today, speaking to us as he did in the sanctuary at Nazareth, would that be sedative? My word!

If someone here deeply needs inner serenity, I hope that something in this service may minister to his want, saying, like Christ
himself: "Peace I leave with you; my peace I give unto you."
But Christian worship means more than peace; it is not a lullaby,
but a challenge to character. I want some ethical consequences
from our worship here today.

I know a man who now is a recognized scholar, a writer of
significant books, a leader in one of our outstanding churches.
He came to church once, drunk—but not so drunk that day that
he could not recognize his moral need; and, all unbeknownst to

me, that service of worship saw his transformation. I did not hear of it until twenty-five years afterwards, but then he wrote me about the way that day God laid a hand on his life's tiller and he came about on a new tack. Coming to church that Sunday was the decisive turning point of his life.

Something like that could happen here today. After a long ministry, dealing with all the kinds of sinners there are, one fact about them stands out unmistakably. In every one of their lives, there were times when they almost made the great decision that would have saved them the shame and torment of their moral failure—they almost made it, nearly, not quite. They were tempted by evil—yes! But there were times when they were tempted by good, when God and the right almost won the day. Someone here now, facing some moral choice, is in that situation. Don't be a mere temple-trampler this morning! Robert Louis Stevenson's description of what happened to him can be true of you: "I came about like a well-handled ship. There stood at the wheel that unknown steersman whom we call God." That is what coming to church this morning can mean to someone here.

There is a second area, however, where we confront, I suspect, the Bible's most disturbing difficulty with churchgoers. Churchgoing can make people little-minded, bigoted, sectarian, confirming and sharpening their prejudices and fanaticisms.

That was the trouble in the Nazareth synagogue that day when Jesus came back to his home town. He knew those people. He had grown up with them. They went up to the synagogue every sabbath, and came down more narrow-minded and prejudiced than they had been before. Jesus was speaking to their real condition when he preached that day a universal God, Father of all men, whose worship should broaden men's outlook, widen their sympathy, override their racial prejudices, and put an end to their bigotry. He tried to do it as persuasively as he could. He appealed to their own great traditions—many widows in Israel, but Elijah sent to a widow of Sidon, many lepers in Israel but Elisha healed Naaman the Syrian. Could they not see what their own great tradition taught—what the prophet Malachi meant when he cried, "Have we not all one father? hath not one God created us?" But they would have none of it. They threw him out. They wanted their churchgoing to confirm their prejudices. Well, look at our American churches today and see how all too commonly that kind of churchgoing is being reduplicated here.

This is what Jesus was thinking of when later he told the story of the good Samaritan. We think that story beautiful. I never get over my amazement at people who think that parable beautiful. Those who first heard it did not think that. They were horrified at it. For, who was it that passed by on the other side and refused to help the wounded man? The priest and the Levite. Where were they going? Down from the Temple in Jerusalem. They had been to church, but of what going to church ought to mean, they had not the faintest idea. It was a Samaritan, who never went to their church, whom they despised as a heretic from an outlawed race, who really understood what the worship of God means. Make no mistake about it, our Lord could be very severe on churchgoers.

This thing I am talking about now is one of the saddest aspects of Christian history: so much worship that has issued in littleness, bitterness, prejudice, so much worship that has supported the worst social sins and national evils. Can you think of anything much more manifestly unchristian than slavery? Yet in the days of slavery in this nation, people often went to church,

North and South, and heard Christianity used in defense of it. Listen to one quotation from a Christian churchman in those days: "American slavery is not only not a sin, but is especially commanded by God through Moses, and approved by Christ through his Apostles." See how churchgoing can be used to back up and confirm our worst! As one of our theologians put it: "Religion is a dangerous drug unless it is wisely administered."

In South Africa today the Rev. Dr. Malan, lately Prime Minister, standing for a racial policy that seems to us utterly unchristian, goes to his church and comes out again with all his bigotries and prejudices confirmed. Well, does nothing like that happen in our American churches?

One of our outstanding American ministers, Howard Thurman, once talked with Gandhi and asked him, "What is the greatest enemy that Jesus Christ has in India?" and Gandhi answered in one word. "Christianity," he said. That sounds dreadful, but, before we brush it off, think about it! Doesn't Christ face some of the worst enemies of his gospel in bigoted, prejudiced, narrow-minded, small-spirited Christianity? Isn't he still saying to us in the church, "Not every one that saith unto me, Lord, Lord . . . but he that doeth the will of my Father who is in heaven"?

Some of us, I am sure, are saying now, Well, this does not apply to us here. So may God grant! But it must apply to millions of us American churchgoers—ninety million of us in the churches and synagogues, and yet look at the religious intolerance, the bitterness, the bigoted sectarianism, the racial prejudices! We too desperately need the God whom Jesus preached in Nazareth —the God of Sidonians and Syrians too, the universal God, whose worship ought to send us out bigger souls not smaller, all-inclusive in our understanding and compassion, not more sectarian and provincial, freed from our intolerant bigotries, not confirmed in them. A woman with two children once came into this church on a Sunday morning and seeing Negroes in the choir stalked out in indignation. Attend a church service where colored people participated—never! Think of that! She little understood what Almighty God was saying to her that morning: "Who hath required this at your hand, to trample my courts?"

This morning I am trying to tempt you. I know that every Sunday we pray, "Lead us not into temptation," but today, if I can possibly manage it, that is precisely where I should like to lead every one of us—into temptation. For it is not alone the seductions of evil which tempt us. No! In our better hours, which ought to come when we worship God together, goodness is tempting too, and decency, and unselfishness, and magnanimity. To do justly, to love mercy, and to walk humbly with our God—that in our better hours can be alluring, tempting, challenging too. When Jesus said to the fishermen of Galilee, "Follow me," he was tempting them. And still the Master is the most tireless tempter of our race, generation after generation appealing to us in our personal lives and our societies to follow him.

God alone knows what youth may be here this morning, facing now, like Isaiah, a call divine which would make history if he should surrender to it. Jesus was only twelve years old when he went up to the Temple, but something happened there which mankind never can forget. He came to a great conviction there. "Wist ye not that I must be about my Father's business?" That kind of experience could happen here this morning.

Ah, Lord! What kind of churchgoer am I?

Things That Never Wear Out

In lines familiar to us all Wordsworth celebrated his delight in a rainbow:

> My heart leaps up when I behold
> A rainbow in the sky:
> So was it when my life began;
> So is it now I am a man;
> So be it when I shall grow old,
> Or let me die!

That is to say, the kind of experience represented in the love of nature with a rainbow in the sky is not spoiled by the attrition of time. A boy can begin it and an old man can still find there fresh delight.

Whether old or young, the range of truth thus suggested ought to be important to us. The wear and tear of time are obvious. If we older ones feel that more poignantly, you younger ones with your eyes open must see it too. For there are not many experiences, are there? concerning which one can say,

> So was it when my life began;
> So is it now I am a man;
> So be it when I shall grow old.

We are not going to say this morning that the worth and joy of life lie altogether in such experiences. As there are seasonal fruits which one does not expect to have growing in one's orchard all the year around, so there are seasonal experiences, peculiar each to a special period of life, to be rejoiced in then even though they cannot be continued. There are experiences peculiar to childhood which, after childhood passes, never will come back again, and ardors and romances in youth which, after youth is gone, will not return. But while this seasonal nature of life is true and the recognition of it important, lest being now youths we still cling to our childhood or, being now adults, we refuse with disastrous psychological results to give up the experiences of youth, yet how much of the depth and richness of life lies in this other realm, in experiences like Wordsworth's with nature, which we can start in childhood and then go on with all our life long to the end!

We may illustrate our meaning first from the very realm which Wordsworth himself suggests. Alas for the child who is not early introduced to the love of nature! Something is lost from that child's life that never can be made up. For *there* is an experience which, no matter how long one lives, never need wear out. How many of us are thankful that early in childhood we fell in love with trees and hills and brooks and flowers, which all the years since have been true friends to us! The vicissitudes of the passing decades have been many and sometimes difficult but always the friendship of nature, steadying, healing, comforting, has been there. Why do we not speak of this more often in our churches—this spiritual ministry of nature to those who love her, this literal meaning of the Psalm?

> He maketh me to lie down in green pastures;
> He leadeth me beside still waters.
> He restoreth my soul.

Indeed, this experience is of profound importance to religion. One of the most powerful influences that have played with dire effect upon religion in recent generations has been city life. How can a person who lives merely in a city and, like some Manhattanites, who are said never to come north of Fourteenth Street, be profoundly religious? Everything he sees is man-made. He swims, as it were, in a sea of man's inventions and creations. What is there in the mechanical externalities which environ him to suggest God? Whenever religion vitally survives in the city, you will find souls, I think, who are not simply city-made but are at home with mountains and woods and the sea and the open sky, that vast background of nature's wonder and mystery which man did not create and before which he is still a little child.

The Bible, for example, the supreme book of religion, is also one of the great books of nature. At its best the Old Testament sprang from the out-of-doors, where

> The heavens declare the glory of God;
> And the firmament showeth his handiwork.

As for the New Testament, while Paul was a city man and said little of nature, Jesus came from the countryside, and one who has been in Galilee in springtime, when the flowers are clothed more gorgeously than Solomon in all his glory, feels how deep in nature was the rootage of his faith in God, who "hath made everything beautiful in its time." Surely, it was no accident that when the end came and the supreme struggle of Jesus' soul was upon him,

> Into the woods my Master went.

This fellowship with nature one can begin as a little child. Although one live ever so long it will not wear out. John Burroughs was one of the great nature lovers of our country. On his eighty-third birthday he said to a circle of friends at a house party, "I have had a happy life. My work has been my play, and I don't want a better world than this to play in, or better men and women for my friends."

Consider another illustrative experience which we can begin in childhood and which never need wear out, the love of reading. Many here remember as one of the earliest reminiscences of home the excitement and fascination of reading—first books read to us and then books read by us. Here was an experience opening before our childhood's astonished eyes, new and strange and marvelous, and with this significance also which then we did not understand—that always books would be our friends.

Why do we not speak of this oftener in the churches? Reading is so influential in our lives! So many of the turning points in man's spiritual history have been caused by it, as with St. Augustine hearing the voice in the garden, "Take up and read," or as with Luther rising up from study of the Epistle to the Galatians to shake Europe with his proclamation of the gospel's freedom! Many a perplexing question about Paul we do not know the answer to, but this we know, that he was a great reader. For in his last imprisonment in Rome, with the end almost at hand, he wrote to his young friend Timothy, "Bring when thou comest . . . the books, especially the parchments." Ah, Paul, we cannot always understand your theology, but we understand that!

To be sure, we for whom the printing press has made reading the common habit of every day often use trivially this great resource. We read to keep up with our professional or business specialties. But a man who uses books in this way only, as

Pharaoh used slaves to build his pyramids, does not know what real reading means. Or we read to keep up with the swiftly moving times—newspapers, magazines, books, pouring in an endless flood from the presses. But a man who uses reading in this way only misses what real reading means. He never would read Homer, which is hardly a means of keeping up with the times, and then, like Keats, say about it afterwards:

> Then felt I like some watcher of the skies
> When a new planet swims into his ken.

Or again, we read because other people read and because we are expected to read the books they are talking of. Of all social coercions nothing is much more compulsive than the exclamation, "What! have you not read so-and-so?" I celebrate today another and higher kind of experience, the spiritual friendship of great books intently read, deeply pondered, one of the abiding experiences of life which a child begins and an old man still gets his comfort from. So said Charles Kingsley—"Except a living man, there is nothing more wonderful than a book!" So said Milton—"A good book is the precious life-blood of a master spirit."

Now, with these two illustrations in mind, the love of nature and the friendship of books, consider that the seasonal experiences of life, fitted to one period only of our existence, constitute our foreground, so important that life grows ill if it be not well handled, but that the background of life, its depth and horizon and enduring worth, comes from this other kind of experience which we can begin in childhood and go through with to the very end. I raise the question: How many things do we possess of this enduring kind?

For example, consider a clear conscience as belonging to this category. A child can enter into that experience and an old man deeply needs it. Some of us were reared in families where internal conscientiousness, not external regimentation, was the reliance of the home. I can remember yet the first time I tried as a boy to cover up a piece of crookedness and felt the appalling inner misery of an accusatory conscience. Long years afterward, when I read Coleridge's description of what an outraged conscience can do to a man, I remembered that childhood's experience—

> Like one, that on a lonesome road
> Doth walk in fear and dread,
> And having once turned round walks on,
> And turns no more his head;
> Because he knows, a frightful fiend
> Doth close behind him tread.

When one pleads for a kind of life that leaves the conscience unashamed, one is commonly understood to be talking morals. But today I am thinking rather of the fact that as a man grows older few things so help him to stand up under hardship as does an unashamed conscience. Standing the gaff as the years pass is not in itself easy but if, in addition to the natural gainsayings and limitations of aging life, a man has to live inwardly with a nasty conscience, how does he stand it? Not simply for the sake of what is commonly called morals but for the sake of a livable life I should say to youth as Phillips Brooks did:

To keep clear of concealment, to keep clear of the need of concealment, to do nothing which he might not do out on the middle of Boston Common at noonday—I cannot say how more and more that seems to me to be the glory of a young man's life.

Indeed, we have spoken so far as though only lovely things—delight in nature, the friendship of books, and a good conscience—carried through to the end. But, of course, other things also carry through. Some sins are like recurring decimals: three into ten, three times and one over, then three into ten, three times and one over, and yet once more, three into ten, three times and one over. Who has not seen some things begun in youth whose consequences go on and on like that? But while in one sense sin does thus carry through, in another sense, how it wears out! How it passes from expectation through committal into memory and never is desirable again! As the years pass, as much as any other thing, an unashamed conscience makes life worth living.

> So was it when my life began;
> So is it now I am a man;
> So be it when I shall grow old.

Consider also that deep interest in intellectual and social causes belongs to this category. I well remember the fascinated hours in boyhood when my father told me of my grandsire's house with its secret closet where escaping slaves were concealed until they could be rowed on dark nights across the Niagara River to Canada and liberty. There to a small boy's fascinated imagination was a strange new interest—a social cause that had cost danger and sacrifice, not finished even yet, which our fathers served and then handed on to us, as though we too should have a hand in making a freer world. Such are some of the great hours in childhood.

Now as the years pass and age comes on, he who enters ever more deeply into this experience—until he lives not simply in himself but in great interests, intellectual and social, more important than himself—is preparing an enriched old age. I do not mean necessarily an easy old age. He may be stricken in body and estate. If he lives long enough, as Holmes said,

> . . . the names he loved to hear
> Have been carved for many a year
> On the tomb.

But as the years pass, a woman like Jane Addams, for example—interested in everything worth being interested in—though she grew old could not by any one be pitied. The whole background of such a life is steady, the continuous experience of living in and for something more than oneself that begins in childhood and ends only with the grave.

Here again our plea is made, you see, not simply in the name of morals. Selfishness is immoral. Yes, but, may a minister say it? selfishness is even more than that.

> The wretch, concentred all in self,
> Living, shall forfeit fair renown,
> And, doubly dying, shall go down
> To the vile dust, from whence he sprung,
> Unwept, unhonored, and unsung.

That kind of trouble with selfishness, which Sir Walter Scott felt—that it makes man a "wretch, concentred all in self"—is nearer our concern today. Self-centeredness peters out. Time corrodes it. It has no enduring quality. Under it one shrivels up at last. The years do devastating things to the man who lives by it. Only the other day I had a letter from a man who confessed to an absorbingly self-centered life and now at sixty wanted me to tell him how on earth he could make life seem worth going on with.

As we see the years pass over us and old age coming on, do we not all feel one desire? We want to be no mere slaves of time.

We do not want to be utterly at the mercy of the calendar. We want something about us that time and tide cannot touch. And here plainly is something—great interests more important than oneself that one lives in and cares for, that were before we came and will be afterwards—treasures, Jesus called them, treasures which neither moth nor rust doth consume, nor thieves break through and steal.

Consider also a deep, interior, spiritual life, grounded in faith in God and sustained by a sense of divine companionship, as belonging to this category. A child can begin that and an old man deeply needs it. In this regard religion is like music, an experience to which, in ways simple yet profound, a child responds, and which, if we are fortunate, lasts and grows through all the years, to be the comfort and sustenance of age.

How profoundly we do need these enduring experiences! For modern life is full of rapid turnovers. Probably life always was like that, but machine industry has accentuated it, so that now things are deliberately made to be worn out and thrown away. And when from physical things we look to psychological experience, there too the same principle exists. For our emotional life is played on by the swift and transient impact of passing sensations through newspapers, movies, radio, television and what not, deliberately designed to produce what we call a "kick" and then be done with, so that, if we do not beware, our lives become mere immediacies and sensationalisms. And if these two towering perils of modern living, immediacy and sensationalism, rule us, then transiency besets everything and a certain meaningless discontinuity takes all abiding significance from life.

Today we are trying to get clearly in our view another range of experience, not aristocratic and reserved for the few, not costing much in money, rather the most democratic and accessible of all experiences—the love of nature, the companionship of books, the unashamed conscience of a good character, the great interests of man's common weal, music, the interior resources of a spiritual life, the lasting experiences that are not merely periodic but go with us across all the years from childhood to the grave.

A profound religious experience—"I live; yet not I, but Christ liveth in me"—does belong to that category. To be sure, plenty of things about religion are periodic and face a rapid turnover. Over a century ago Andover Theological Seminary was founded and in the dogmatic spirit of the time a creed was laid down as its foundation concerning which the fathers of the institution said, "Every article of the abovesaid Creed shall forever remain entirely and identically the same, without the least alteration, or any addition or diminution." Well, that creed lasted about seventy-five years and then its final defender was called "the dauntless soldier of a forlorn hope." Plenty of things about religion face a rapid turnover.

The religious experience itself, the deep and inward sense of a divine companionship, however, is like the love of nature or of music, one of the enduring things. Some of us, remembering back, think we understand at least a little what Jesus meant when he took children in his arms and as the second Gospel says, "laying his hands upon them," he talked to his disciples about the kingdom of God in terms of a child's spirit. The Gospel of Thomas is one of the "lost gospels" and of it we have left only a few pages. One of its sayings is a quotation from Jesus—"He that seeketh me shall find me in children from seven years old onwards, for there I am manifested." There are some of us on whom he laid his hands when we were about as young as that, and now as older years come on we bear witness to an abiding experience of divine companionship that holds life together, gives it resources of power, and makes sense of it.

> So was it when my life began;
> So is it now I am a man;
> So be it when I shall grow old.

Throughout this sermon I have not been quite sure whether I was talking more to the older people or to the young, but now at the close I know. I want a word especially with the young. Often when an older man talks to you, you think he does not know your problem, has forgotten what youth was like, or does not understand that youth today faces a situation far different from his long-past generation, and in this you doubtless are often justified. But now I am not talking about being young; I am talking about growing old. And you may not say that we do not know about that; *that* is something we do know about.

And we are saying that as the years pass you are going to want the enduring experiences. For your happiness, then, if for no other reason, get them now. All these things we have spoken of, from the love of nature to the inward divine companionship, are easy to possess when one is young. Is it not as natural as breathing for children to know them all if they have half a chance? But when the years have passed and all one's days have been expended on the transient and the merely seasonal in human life, then it is not easy. Then one wakes up to discover how much he needs the abiding treasures of experience, concerning which one can say: "As it was in the beginning, is now, and ever shall be, world without end. Amen."

Redigging Old Wells[1]

Iᴛ is fortunate that special occasions like Memorial Day inter-
rupt our merely individual choice of sermon themes. Whether
we will or not, these occasions call us back to areas of experience
and thought which, following too much the devices and desires
of our own hearts, as the prayer book says, we might not light
upon. In particular, Memorial Day recalls the heritage of our
sires and their sacrifices, and makes us re-estimate our responsibility to the inheritance that they have handed down to us. Let
us quicken and vivify our imagination of the day's significance
by turning to an old narrative recorded for us in the Book of
Genesis. "Isaac," the story reads, "digged again the wells of
water, which they had digged in the days of Abraham his father;
for the Philistines had stopped them after the death of Abraham:
and he called their names after the names by which his father
had called them."

We have here the record of the recovery of an old gain that
had been lost. With wells of living water the sons of the desert
are rich; without them they are hopeless. So when Isaac and
his family returned to the old places where Abraham had lived,
their first concern was the rediscovery of the wells which Abraham had digged. What had happened is clearly stated for us:
"All the wells which his father's servants had digged in the days

[1] A Memorial Day sermon.

of Abraham his father, the Philistines had stopped, and filled with earth."

Put yourself, then, in Isaac's place. His father had done good work which now had been undone by the Philistines. Quite apart from the practical and urgent need of water, his filial loyalty must have been touched. He digged again the wells which his father had digged and he called them by the names by which his father had called them. How relevant this story is to our contemporary situation! Two kinds of duty constantly face us, and in this world all true progress depends on both— new gains to be made and old gains to be rewon; new wells to be dug and old wells that have been stopped to be dug again. Fresh things to do and old things to be recovered—both make up life.

Anyone who understands the trend and temper of our time will be aware that some will be reluctant to face this latter aspect of the truth. Some young, eager spirits here may shrug their shoulders, saying, Going back to old gains to be rewon is a reactionary process about which I am not concerned; I am a liberal; I am a progressive; I say, Let us go forward; this redigging of old wells is not my business. To which I answer, I am a liberal, too, and just because we are liberals we would better give particular heed to this lesson which Memorial Day suggests and which so much of our experience confirms. It is dangerously easy to cheapen the meaning of great words, and liberalism is no exception.

Beethoven was a liberal in music. More than any other man in his time, he blazed trails which music has followed since. If you ask why he was so successful an innovator, you will find the critics agreed on one point; no man in his day compared with him in the range and accuracy of his information about everything that had been done or tried in music before him. Almost all successful progress comes from those who know best and most deeply appreciate the achievements that have gone before them. Whenever liberalism lacks this element it inevitably grows thin and tenuous, shallow and cheap.

Owen Wister once told us that in Philadelphia a woman went into a library and asked for one of the new books. Handed a volume, she soon returned it with undisguised contempt. "But," she said, "that book was written over a year ago. I asked for a new book." Shades of the spacious days of great Elizabeth! No book worth reading that is over a year old! Yet in many a realm besides reading, plenty of moderns are tempted to such cheap and superficial modernity.

In contrast, then, on the threshold of Memorial Day, let us study the character of Isaac. He seems to have been a man of fine quality. We read, for example, "and Isaac went out to meditate in the field at the eventide." You see the sort of man he was. He had spiritual resources. He had a rich inner life. Solitude was not irksome to him. He loved to be alone, and when darkness fell and the Syrian night of many stars came down upon the desert he walked abroad and felt the presence that disturbed him with the joy of elevated thoughts.

Moreover, in all ancient literature no love story compares with the romance of Isaac and Rebekah. You who are weary of the sordid, morbid, sex-ridden love tales of today, go back and read again the twenty-fourth chapter of Genesis and see if it is not like coming out of the fetid air of slums into the clean breezes of the mountains. Even yet, millenniums afterwards, in the Episcopal ritual we hear the clergyman marry our friends with desire that they may have a love like that which bound together

Isaac and Rebekah, and across the centuries one's recollections are carried back by that ritual from this modern world to an old and simple time and the restrained language of a fine romance: "Isaac took Rebekah, and she became his wife; and he loved her."

This impression of Isaac as a man of elevated sentiment and fine quality is confirmed by the special text of the morning. He had had Abraham for his father and he gloried in it. He honored the place where his father had lived; he loved the things that his father had loved. He did not live merely on this narrow neck of land that we call the present. He honored the past. He felt the sacredness of its heritage and the worth of its spiritual gains.

Some people are merely contemporary, merely modern. They seem to live upon the shallow puddle gathered from the rain that chanced to fall last night. But others know about the sea, the accumulated gains of all the rains that ever fell upon the earth, and they know what it means to leave at times the shallow pool of last night's chance shower and go down beside the ancient ocean, look out across its breadth and depth, and refresh and establish themselves in communion with the past. Such a man was Isaac. He could have kept Memorial Day.

While, however, this attitude of his was a fine sentiment, it was not idle and inoperative. It struck fire on a specific situation. It involved him in laborious toil. He found something that his fathers had done that had been undone by the Philistines. He digged again the wells that his father had digged. Can we make our keeping of Memorial Day thus an effective and serviceable thing? Millions of Americans will feel the sentiments proper to the day. Flowers on the graves of our beloved dead, songs of memory for all the saints who from their labors rest, feelings of gratitude for the sacrifices by which our securities and safeties have been purchased—well and good! But, after all, the deepest tribute to our sires is not sentiment but the recovery of old gains they made which the Philistines have stolen. Dig again the wells which the Philistines have stopped! That is not an ancient story. Look around you and see!

In the first place, let us apply this truth to our personal character. There are multitudes of personal characters to which it does apply. Here, for example, comes word from one of our younger generation as quoted in the *Atlantic Monthly*: "I'm getting to the end of things I want to do. I've done all the things I've been told not to—and they aren't so amusing as they looked. There's a screw loose somewhere. . . . Suppose we were to pick out somebody who is decent and find out what it is about him." Suppose we should! Suppose we should go back and redig some old wells!

This necessity of recovery as part of the process of every good life must be clear to all of us. How familiar the experience is! We plunge on, month after month, in a preoccupied life, hurried, restless, trying effectively to do a thousand new things, and then suddenly comes a pause. It may be that illness lays us low for an interval and we have time to take stock. It may be that some vacation in the mountains or beside the sea gives us opportunity to relax, let down, reorient ourselves, get new horizons around our lives. It may be that some music stirs reminiscent chords for long untouched or that some sermon wakens echoes of old teachings heard long since and long forgotten and, lo! something old and deep and fundamental rises in us. We are called back to something that we ought never to have forgotten. My friends, much of what we call progress is not progress; it is restoration. It is the re-emergence in us of something very old. It is the redigging of ancient wells.

How interesting in this regard the work of memory is! When Abraham and Isaac lived together they doubtless had hours of strain. There were times when Isaac was petulant or undutiful and Abraham was harsh—they were human—but now, when Isaac remembers Abraham, all that is forgotten. Ever as Isaac remembers him, Abraham grows more admirable. So on the surface of the Nile there are back eddies and cross currents, but when one has sailed up and down it he does not remember them. He only recalls that majestic river flowing with steadfast and fructifying purpose from the mountains to the sea. So Isaac remembered Abraham. Blessed is the work of memory upon our friends! We call it idealizing them, but that is not the whole truth. Only the nonessentials fall away and their major meaning, their substantial beauty, stands clear. "As we recede from them, the hills descend, the mountains rise." How many of us here this morning, in the background of our lives, have fathers, mothers, children, friends towering up mountainous and clear in cleansing memory! Truly to keep Memorial Day is to let these sacred recollections have their way with us. You say it is sentiment. I am not disturbed by that. Some sentiments are worth dying for. But it need not be an idle, inoperative sentiment.

Was it nothing to the prodigal son in the far country, friends gone, money gone, forced to the companionship of swine, that out in the fields that day he began to remember? What an unworthy contrast between his present squalor and his home, as memory pictured it to him! What living wells his father had digged in him that the Philistines had filled up! That memory was not an idle thing. It was terrific. It scourged him with shame and then beckoned him with irresistible allurement. Can some of us keep Memorial Day so? I do not know what wells of living water the Philistines in New York City have been trying to fill up in your lives but I know that no one of us can fail in some degree to share this universal experience. We need to be called back to things that we have loved long since and lost awhile.

Therefore, let wholesome, cleansing, saving memories play on you today! Let them call you back to things you ought not to have forgotten—to God, to purity, to honesty, to service, to prayer. Dig again the wells your fathers dug!

This truth applies not simply to personal character but to personal religion. As with everything else, so with religion; if it is to command its generation it must have in it things both new and old. Timeliness and eternity are both indispensable to a powerful religion. Our Christianity must meet us today where we are in this modern world, with our special circumstances and our contemporary modes of thought. And, at the same time, our Christianity must be as old as the human heart, with its abiding needs and aspirations. Indeed, it is this necessity of combining the old and the new in religion that creates so much of our present American problem with it.

The same is true about poetry. Rereading a fascinating book by Professor J. Livingstone Lowes on *Convention and Revolt in Poetry* I was interested to discover in how many passages I could insert "religion" for "poetry" and have the literary critic's words hold true. For poetry, like religion, has its florescent periods, its Elizabethan epochs, when it bursts forth with creative energy, breaking through old forms and channeling new thoroughfares for the spirit. Then it becomes conventional. Lesser souls take the old forms, in which the fire and fury of creative genius have been extinguished, and put words into them. You have in consequence a time of conventional formalism, frigid conceits instead of fortunate eloquence. Old forms of poetry move about like so many suits of clothes walking down Broadway with nobody in them.

Out of such an age of formalism, surely Professor Lowes is right in saying that mankind always finds two ways of escape. Some write free verse; they use rhythms never before tried or no rhythms at all; they seek release in novelty and modernism. And some go back to the old forms, lift them up, revivify them, pour genius and passion into them, make them live and sing and soar again. So, Rupert Brooke, in the First World War, wanting to speak his heart out, took an old sonnet form and poured passion into it:

> If I should die, think only this of me:
> That there is some corner of a foreign field
> That is forever England.

Who of us, then, would not agree with Professor Lowes about the value of these two ways of dealing with a conventional period? Is not free verse useful? Of course it is. "Fresh beginnings are excellent stimulants to a jaded world," he says. And is it not good to preserve the values of the old traditions? Of course it is. "Cut," he says, "the connection with the great reservoir of past achievement, and the stream runs shallow, and the substance of poetry becomes tenuous and thin."

That double lesson is deeply needed by American religion. If I were speaking to fundamentalists today I would talk like this: What can you mean by thinking that you can get at the mind and heart of this generation if you do not live in the new world of thought and life where this generation lives? See how like hermit crabs you crawl into cast-off creedal shells of dead ancestors and ensconce yourselves there while all the time those shells were not built out of the living juices of your own spirits and do not represent the vital forces of this generation. You are afraid of new truth and that is arch infidelity against the living God, to whom new truth as well as old belongs.

However, I am not talking to fundamentalists. I am talking in a church committed to liberal positions. We are not afraid of the new; we are far more likely to forget the old, and no good thing in this world is ever done except by a combination of the new and the old. This is true even about airplanes. To us older folk one of the most exciting occasions which we remember will always be the day Charles Lindbergh flew the ocean. That was something brand new, full of promise and portent, a prophetic event foretelling a changed world. But it was not simply brand new. Something old was there too—personal courage, venturesome faith. Beneath all that was new in that flight, the very substance and sustenance of it, were old qualities of character which have brought to human history from the beginning its sublimest hours.

I am not afraid of your attitude toward the new in our interpretations and applications of Christian truth. You are not frightened at modernity. You are ready to tackle new tasks and face new thoughts and you are not going to "attempt the future's portal with the Past's blood-rusted key." But modernity by itself is not enough. It takes the profound experiences of vital religion to make a genuine Christian. And they are not new. They are old. They were in Jesus and Paul and St. Francis and Luther and John Wesley. They lie underneath all the changes of the passing centuries in custom and opinion. They spring from the soul's deep, inward devotion to spiritual values; they are rooted in the spirit's fellowship with the living God.

Some of you came here this morning to hear a modernist

preacher. Will you recall, then, what this modernist preacher says? He tells you that in many a liberal spirit the Philistines have choked up some fine wells that our fathers digged: prayer, that makes the Divine our unseen companion; faith that we came forth from God and are going unto God; power, strengthened with might by God's Spirit in the inner man; personal devotion to the cause of Jesus Christ as the organizing center of life; conviction that a kingdom of righteousness is possible here on earth and determination to put that first and all other things second—old wells to dig again. And if we do not redig them and keep them clear, all our modernism will be futile.

We must hasten, however, to our final application, made inevitable by our national holiday. For these wells which Abraham digged were not merely an individual possession of Isaac's; they were a public benefaction. Every caravan that passed that way called down the blessings of God Almighty on the man who redug those wells. They were a social gift, and Isaac was about a piece of business indispensable in every generation when he dug again the wells that his fathers had dug.

How can a man look at America today and not see the inevitable application of this truth? To be sure, our pet and prevalent word is progress. It is our prescription for almost all our evils. If we find ourselves in any ill situation, we say we will progress out of it. There is indispensable truth in that attitude. Progress is real. Some places we never will escape from except by progressing into something new. The urgency of international living, for example, inevitably will play upon this nation as upon all nations, force ever more upon us the reconsideration of our historic attitude, make international life more important to us and international organization more inevitable. Not only the pull of ideals but the push of necessity has already brought us to the United Nations and far beyond that lie the possibilities of an integrated humanity.

While, however, it is true that progress alone can save us from some things, who can suppose that that is all we need? New wells alone will not save this nation; some old wells must be dug again. One thinks of that as he watches our divorces mount, and our family life disintegrate before our eyes. Nothing that we call progress will get us out of that, only the re-emergence in us of something very old: unselfishness in love, purity, self-control and decency re-established as ideals of character, genuine devotion to family life and to the care of children—old wells to dig again.

One thinks of that as he sees the constant assaults on free speech in America, the dangerous drift toward supine conformity, the smear campaigns, the imitations of communist thought-control by those who profess to be fighting communism. Nothing that we call progress will reverse that trend—only the restoration in us of our fathers' love of independence and liberty, their belief in freedom to think, and their determination in a democracy to say what, by God's grace, they see fit to say about the public weal.

One thinks of this as he sees the filth that like an open sewer flows through some of our reading matter—not alone its pornographic and horror comics—until one of our leading citizens has said that our children will look back on our time and call it "the dirty decade." Nothing that we call progress will get us out of that—only the re-emergence in us of something old: self-respect, decency, disgust at things contemptible and low, public revulsion against panderers who grow financially fat on the exploitation of vice.

One thinks of this as he watches America living prosperously and sees the inevitable temptations that therefore play on all of us. How clear it is that if America is really going forward it must go back, back to some things old and fine, familiar and fundamental. In my callow youth I reached the conclusion that we had so far spiritually progressed that we could center all attention on Paul's positive ethic, "Love is the fulfilling of the law," and that we need no longer stress the negative "Thou shalt not." I take it back. I know human life better. I wish those Ten Commandments could be blazoned in every market place, in every schoolhouse, in every church.

> Thou shalt not kill.
> Thou shalt not commit adultery.
> Thou shalt not steal.
> Thou shalt not bear false witness.
> Thou shalt not covet—

old wells to dig again!

My friends, on Memorial Day your hearts will be occupied with the sentiments of memory. Some of you may even go back to Arlington, above the still Potomac, and review in reminiscence the brave men who, a long generation ago, fought their fight for liberty and union. Some of you, whose eyes have not yet been taught to stay dry, will think of the men and women who fell in the world wars. Let such memories dwell in your hearts, but deeper still go back to the basic faiths and virtues which at their best distinguished our fathers, and without which in us our fathers' sacrifices will be vain. Old wells to dig! God forbid that the Philistines should stop them and fill them up with earth!

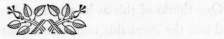

Things That Money Cannot Buy

ONE of our American journalists, a practical, hard-headed man, has said, "It is a good thing to have money and the things that money can buy, but it is a good thing to check up once in a while and make sure you have not lost the things that money cannot buy."

In a sense there is nothing new about that. Long ago Isaiah cried to his people, "He that hath no money; come ye, buy, and eat; yea, come, buy wine and milk without money and without price." Long ago Jesus pled for the unpurchasable treasures of the spirit that moth and rust cannot consume nor thieves break through and steal. Nevertheless, while this emphasis on the things that money cannot buy is not new, there is urgent contemporary need of its recovery. Ours is one of the most financially-minded eras in history. All our major problems are conceived in economic terms. Our popular Utopia is commonly pictured as an epoch when everybody will be financially well-to-do, and even theories of economic determinism guarantee to explain everything that ever has happened in history or ever will. With the monetary aspect of affairs thus bulking large in our social fears, endeavors and hopes, personal money-mindedness, which has always been the chief form of man's idolatry, gains a fresh dominance. I am not now viewing with alarm; I am trying objectively to state a plain fact about our generation. We are obsessed with the economic aspect of life.

Where else, if not in the church, shall the other side of the matter be presented? It is a good thing to check up once in a while and make sure that you have not lost the things that money cannot buy.

Certainly, that is true in the family. The monetary underpinning of a household is profoundly important. Alas! The wreckage of romantic hopes, the devastation of domestic love, the ruin of childhood's chances that come from the lack in the home of the things that money can buy! Nevertheless, you know homes, some rich, some poor, some financially average. Can you on that basis decide where the greatest wreckage of family life appears or where the full tide of love and fidelity runs highest? I can remember my mother, under economic pressure, weeping because once more she had to lower another notch the level of expenditures in our family, but I had a lovely home. And I see today households with everything cash can get that in comparison awaken my pity or disgust. Granted the importance of purchasable things to the family, yet in the long run it is the things that money cannot purchase, listed in no market, rated on no exchange, that determine what the family will really be.

Surely, this is true inside personal life. Here is a restless, irritable, aimless man, without peace, without poise, weak in temptation, unstable in strain; and here is a man of another kind altogether, a dependable character—you can count on him. Can you deduce from that difference between two men their economic status? Stability cannot be bought. As Robert Burns said,

> It's no in titles nor in rank;
> It's no in wealth like Lon'on Bank,
> To purchase peace and rest.

In pressing home this side of the case, we are almost sure to lay ourselves open to grave misunderstanding. Someone is bound to think that we are minimizing the importance of economic conditions. Let us get that matter straightened out in advance as far as we can. It is foolish to underrate the importance of economic conditions. In our modern life money is not simply money; it is food to eat and a roof over our heads, education for the children, books and music and trips to the mountains and the seaside. It is help for those we love in time of need, and expectancy of old age relieved from haunting fear. It is foolish indeed to minimize life's economic subsoil. Moreover, some of our dearest social liberties are rooted in it. We say this is a free country, but political freedom is not enough. Many people are not free—not free from the deadly dread of penury, not free to do for their children what as American fathers and mothers they would make any sacrifice to do, not free to avail themselves of the level of subsistence and opportunity around them, not free from crushing anxiety today and paralyzing fear of unemployment and old age tomorrow. And free speech, free press, free assembly, free ballot—priceless as they are—are a poor makeshift for a man who lacks economic freedom.

Moreover, when one thinks of the world at large facing the threat of war and sees how basic in this situation are the economic factors, it would be preposterous to minimize them. There is an old fable about an ox and a colt that went to a spring to drink and then fell to quarreling as to which should drink first. There was plenty of room for them to drink together, but, nonetheless, they quarreled bitterly about precedence and were preparing to fight it out when, looking up, they saw the vultures wheeling low above them, waiting for the battle and its aftermath. So, says the fable, they decided to drink together. Well, the vultures are flying low over the world today. They have picked the bones of previous civilizations that fought it out, and they may pick ours yet. As one sees how basic in this threatening situation are the economic factors, one would be senseless to minimize them.

Today, however, we are saying that everybody is thinking *this*. We cannot open the morning paper without running on it. Our contemporary books are full of it. It is the towering concern and obsession of our time. It is the other side of the matter that is crowded out. It is a good thing to have money and the things that money can buy but is *that* emphasis needed here today? "Man," said Jesus, "man shall not live by bread alone"— that thought is crowded out. Treasures that moth and rust cannot consume nor thieves break through and steal—they are crowded out.

In the first place, then, consider that the deepest differences between persons lie in the things that money cannot purchase. Here, for example, is a cynic. He sees no sense in life. Thomas Hardy told the story, moving and tragic, of *Tess of the D'Urbervilles*, and ended by saying over the baffled career and sorry death of the unfortunate girl, "The President of the Immortals (in Aeschylean phrase) had ended his sport with Tess." That, thinks the cynic, is life's proper summary, and for an epitaph he would suggest for his tombstone,

> Don't bother me now, don't bother me never.
> I want to be dead for ever and ever.

Here on the other side is a far different sort of man, who has kept his zest. Life for him has been hard enough, tragic even, but it has had meaning. He might even say with Epictetus,

"Bring whatever you please, and I will turn it into *good*," or with Paul, "To them that love God all things work together for good," and as for his epitaph, it is far different from the cynic's, for at his life's end he says, "I have fought the good fight, I have finished the course, I have kept the faith."

That difference between men who keep their zest and those who lose it is one of the most significant in human experience. If some youth here has not yet found that difference important, he will sometime. What a difference there is between those for whom life grows ever emptier and those for whom life grows ever fuller of meaning! You cannot explain that difference in terms of anything that money can buy. A cynic may die in a palace. Paul died a prisoner. You cannot tell. The great enthusiasts about life, who have faced it as a challenge and rejoiced in it, have commonly dealt with difficult, adverse circumstances. You cannot tell. The deep faiths, the spiritual insights, the inward resources of personal power, the strong companionships of the soul—these factors that make all things work together for good are not for sale, not listed in any market, not rated on any exchange. They move in the unpurchasable realm.

Despite our exaggerated popular theories of economic determinism, this holds, I think, of all the profoundest differences between people. A life burdened by a sense of guilt and shame versus a clear conscience that can look the whole world in the face—what a difference that is! A life that has repelled friendship and ended in embittered isolation versus a life whose genuine goodwill has won affection and surrounded itself with friends; a life inwardly shattered by a sense of inferiority and inadequacy versus a life that has tapped resources of spiritual power until what ought to be done can be done and what must be endured can be finely faced; hopeless living that thinks the

world in the end will go to the dogs, and that each soul at death
passes into oblivion, versus hopeful life sustained by the eternal
purpose which God purposed in Christ—such contrasts constitute the deepest differences between people. And always the
same truth emerges: you cannot buy in any market a clear
conscience or genuine affection or inward spiritual power or
deathless hope. They move in the unpurchasable realm.

If someone says that this is obvious, I say, Yes, but this obvious
thing, this platitude if you will, is by our prevalent obsession with
economic affairs so crowded out that all around us are men and
women who desperately need to check up and make sure that
they have not lost the things that money cannot buy.

Certainly the people who have money need that. Jesus cared
about the poor and constantly emphasized his concern for them,
but Jesus did not worry half so much about the moral estate of
the poor as he did about the moral estate of the rich. He feared
the possession of money as a major moral peril. Why did he
say—as the verse probably read in the original Aramaic that
Jesus spoke—"It is easier for a rope to go through the eye of a
needle, than for a rich man to enter into the kingdom of God"?
Why did he tell the parable about a man of means whose over-
flowing barns met no need when his soul was required of him?
Jesus saw clearly—of that the evidence is all around us—that
money can buy so many things that they who have it are sorely
tempted to forget the things it cannot buy. We are all concerned
about that portion of the American population lacking money
enough for decent livelihood. Were Jesus here he also would be
concerned about that problem of penury. But he would be more
concerned about the moral estate of us who do have money
enough for a decent livelihood.

If we do not take account of this, all our economic utopias

will turn out to be failures. Be sure of that! Emphasize as we will the profound importance of economic justice and affluence for all! We may well emphasize it. But imagine, if you can, a world where monetary abundance belongs to all, everything that cash can get in the hands of all, every man and woman able to say to his soul, "Soul, thou hast much goods laid up for many years; take thine ease, eat, drink, be merry," but where the things that money cannot buy have been neglected, forgotten, lost. What a hell it would be! What a disillusioning aftermath of high ideal and hard work—means without meaning, things without spiritual significance and purpose. Underscore this: *Everything that money can buy depends for its ultimate worth, for the purpose it serves, for its final effect on human life, upon the things that money cannot buy.* There, in the unpurchasable realms of the spirit lie the determinants of human destiny.

In the second place, consider that this truth, if we take it in earnest, throws the responsibility for what our lives are to mean inwardly upon ourselves. Obsession with the economic aspects of life creates the idea that money makes the man, so that if one lacks money one is tempted to think oneself a failure or to blame lack of character on lack of means, or in general to be discouraged and at loose ends. It is hard enough lacking money anyway, but in a generation when so many voices are shouting that poverty is the inevitable cause of insanity, criminality, loose character, ruined homes and general moral dilapidation, it is worse yet. Now, there is enough truth in this prevalent idea to make it undeniable. Poverty does profoundly affect character. Who can know anything about slums and doubt that? Recall the words of the apothecary in *Romeo and Juliet*, where, when against the law he sells the dangerous drug, he says, "My poverty, but not my will, consents." Poverty often is a cause of, more often, I fear, an excuse for, letdown in character.

On the other side, there is a man in this city now, pilloried in public condemnation, a man who was trusted with the highest position in one of the greatest financial institutions of the land, a man of wealth with everything that money could buy. Was it his poverty that consented to his shame? Friends, we cannot tell where great character is coming from, from penury or plenty. Gautama Buddha came from a king's palace. Jesus Christ came from a carpenter's shop. Lincoln and Gladstone emerged at the same time, born in the same year, one with very little that money could buy, the other with practically everything that money could buy, but both with a strong hold on the things that money cannot buy.

I am hoping that someone here may be liberated by this truth from slavery to the economic test as standard and determinative of life. Put it this way: possession is one thing; ownership is another. Some people possess much and own little; some people possess little and own much. Possession concerns things that can be bought and sold; ownership concerns values that money cannot buy. Possession is having a house; ownership is having a home in it. Possession is having a five-hundred-acre estate; ownership is being a real lover of nature. I am not saying these two are unrelated; I am not saying that possession does not matter. I am saying those two things are different. Happy the man who has been inwardly liberated from the too clamorous insistence of possession and who really lives in the wide ranges of spiritual ownership.

Indeed, over against our prevalent test of life by what we possess, I venture to suggest that a far deeper test of life is what we can go without. How much can you go without and still be a real person? That is a test, and it is an unusual life that does not some time have to face it. It is a test even of nations. When Goebbels, the Nazi minister of propaganda, proclaimed to his people, "We can well do without butter, but not without guns," we learned a lot about what was going on in Germany. Within personal life that test is paramount. Helen Keller can go without sight and hearing and be a real person. Dr. Trudeau could go without health for years and be a great person. Kernahan went without arms or legs from birth but sat in Parliament and was a powerful person. Some of the realest persons in this congregation are poor, some very poor. It is an honor to know them. In possession slight, in ownership magnificent, they are shining examples of what one can do without and still be real persons.

Once, so the story runs, there was a prodigy, a young violinist who created a great furor of popular applause. But envious rivals started the rumor that he was not really great in himself, that it was an extraordinary Stradivarius he played upon that made those moving tones which captivated his audience. So one night in London the violinist played his whole program through without leaving the platform and more than ordinarily stirred the great assemblage to thunderous applause; then he took the violin he had been playing on all the evening, smashed it into bits across his knee, and threw it on the floor. "I will now," said he, "play one number on my Strad." His quality was in himself and not merely in an instrument that gold could buy.

Finally, see how straight our truth leads to one of the deepest needs of our generation, the need for a redefinition of success. Our fathers may have cried in earnest, "What must I do to be saved?" but our generation has been reared to cry, What must I do to succeed?

Here, I suspect, is the most difficult problem we face when we try to be really Christian. Here in the church we are supposed to be concerned with things that money cannot buy—faith in God, discipleship to Christ, high quality of character, unselfishness of life, inner resources of power. These unpurchasable treasures of the soul we would get for ourselves and hand on to our children, but out there in the world, what tremendous pressures of ambition and desire move in another direction toward the things that money can buy!

In Plato's *Republic* there is a searching passage where Socrates points out that it is not what youth is privately taught concerning virtue that most influences youth, but what is applauded in the assembly and in the market place. So when our young men and women go from our churches and schools into the assembly and the market place, what a roar of applause greets success defined in economic terms! Indeed, so true is this that men and women easily grow cynical about any other attitude. Said Voltaire, "When it is a question of money, everybody is of the same religion." That is a lie! When it is a question of money all men are not of the same religion. John Milton gave his life to a cause, spent his sight on it, and for writing *Paradise Lost* received ten pounds. Beethoven made a disappointing pittance out of his first performance of the immortal Ninth Symphony. Such men cared first for things creative, beautiful, not for sale. Spinoza, the philosopher, lived in Holland and humbly made a poor livelihood polishing lenses, meanwhile thinking great thoughts about God. Louis XIV offered him a pension and patronage if he would dedicate only one book to his majesty. Spinoza did not believe in Louis XIV, so in poverty he polished lenses and thought great thoughts. A clergyman in New Zealand was told by the ecclesiastical authorities that if he continued his liberal course his salary would be dropped, to which he wrote back, "You can get very good fish here in the bay, and I know a place in the woods where you can dig up roots that you can eat."

When it is a question of money all men are not of the same religion. On that point Judas Iscariot and Jesus Christ were not of the same faith. In a long ministry I have known many a businessman to sacrifice gain, position, and sometimes all apparent promise of an economic future for conscience' sake. Yet the temptation is terrific to say, What must we do to succeed? and then to define success in financial terms. Wanted, men and women not for sale! More than anything else in the world today, in the pulpit, in business, in public life, wanted men and women not for sale! But on only one condition can such men and women come. They must be persons who within themselves have centered and grounded their life in the things that money cannot buy.

Stand for a moment before the cross of Christ! We cannot pay for that, nor for the life that led up to it or the sacrifice that there was consummated. Such a free gift of life moves in the unpurchasable realm. We are the children of such living, its pensioners and beneficiaries, and all our finest benedictions have come thus from lives not for sale. So the whole weight of the gospel presses home our truth. It is a good thing to have money and the things that money can buy, but it is a good thing to check up once in a while and make sure that we have not lost the things that money cannot buy.

Who Do You Think You Are?

CHRISTIAN faith is commonly interpreted in terms of what we think about God and Christ; but to stop there is to leave out a momentous matter with which the New Testament is deeply concerned—namely, what we think about ourselves. Who do you think you really are?—with that question the New Testament confronts us. How important that question is! Some time since a man committed suicide and left a note behind. "I'm not really needed," it said; "nobody gives a hang for me. I'm just a peanut at the Yankee Stadium. I'll step on myself once and for all." Is there anyone here who has not sometime been tempted to think like that about himself?—a peanut at the Yankee Stadium.

The answer which the New Testament gives to the question, Who are we?—the description it offers of us miserable sinners— is as nearly incredible as anything in the Bible. Writes Paul to the Thessalonians, "Ye are all sons of light"; to the Galatians, "Because ye are sons, God sent forth the Spirit of his Son into our hearts"; to the Corinthians, "We are a temple of the living God"; to the Romans, "The Spirit himself beareth witness with our spirit, that we are children of God." And this glowing description which Paul gives of us humans John confirms: "Now are we children of God, and it is not yet made manifest what we shall be." We talk continually of the problem of believing in

God. Well, I believe in God. My difficulty concerns believing the New Testament's estimate of man.

Ours in particular is a generation when it is easy to take a dim view of human nature. Man's wickedness now threatens the very survival of the race. Here, indeed, is the biggest change that has taken place in my lifetime—this swing from the cheerful optimism about man and his prospects, which prevailed in the late nineteenth century, to the grim confrontation of human folly and depravity and the dire foreboding about man's future which prevail today.

To be sure, David in his haste called all men liars; Carlyle said that England was populated mostly by fools; and Mark Twain once remarked, "All I care to know is that man is a human being; that is enough for me—he can't be any worse." Nevertheless, in the years before the two world wars we oldsters did live in an era of optimism about man. What days those were when science began pouring out its new inventions promising to remake the world! Now, however, we grimly wonder what devilish horrors man will perpetrate with his new science, and we hear dismal forebodings about the possibility that with the H-bomb we may commit racial suicide.

What days those were when not only science but universal education seemed a glorious panacea—all that man needed just the release by adequate schooling of what Browning called "the imprisoned splendour" in him. But now is education saving the world? Upon the contrary, one of communist Russia's major achievements is the conquest of illiteracy among its people. Communism believes in education, wants all its people able to read its propaganda, wants all the trained experts it can find to do its bidding. Education is a tool, and what comes of it at last depends on who uses it, what quality of character, what social purposes, what national ambitions get their hands on it.

And what days those were when not only science and education were supposed to be saving the world, but when evolution was interpreted as guaranteeing inevitable progress; when men like Samuel Butler, half a century ago, could predict that inevitably, automatically, because of evolution man's body would become "finer to bear his finer mind, till man becomes not only an angel but an archangel." Well, look at mankind today and try to imagine us automatically evolving into archangels. What nonsense!

So one disillusionment after another about human nature has crashed down on us, dreadfully accentuated by two world wars and their aftermath, until human depravity and folly have become central in our picture of man! And yet, there is the New Testament! Who are we? Temples of the living God; children of God; sons of light; exceeding great and precious promises, that by these ye might be partakers of the divine nature. My soul! How difficult to believe that aspect of the Christian faith!

Plenty of people today do not believe it; they are skeptics, pessimists, cynics. Their difficulty is not so much belief in God as belief in man. Man, says one of our cynics, is "a small but boisterous bit of the organic scum that for the time being coats part of the surface of one small planet." So that is what we are —a small but boisterous bit of organic scum!

Most of us, to be sure, do not really believe that, but we cannot lightly brush off the dreadful lesson which this generation is teaching us about human sinfulness. I am not a cynic, but I am much more realistic about man than I used to be. Man is a sinner; there is truth in that old doctrine of original sin—something fundamentally wrong in us from which we desperately need to be saved, and from which science alone cannot save us, nor education alone, nor any automatic evolution, only what the New Testament calls the grace of God, forgiveness, spiritual rebirth, being inwardly transformed by the renewing of our minds.

If some modern-minded person here is saying, Oh, that is old theology, I say, All right, we will drop theology for a moment and turn to psychiatry. Sigmund Freud was no theologian; he did not believe in God, but he spent his life studying human nature, and see what he found! Inherent in man, deep-rooted in the unconscious, see what he found! He called it the *Id,* a riotous realm of selfish, sensual drives, which the ego and the superego struggle often vainly to control. It is not a pretty picture. Freud himself expressly recognized the kinship between his concept of the *Id* and the old doctrine of original sin. One commentator has even described Freud's disclosures of human nature as like turning over the stone of the human mind and revealing a great population of ugly insects scuttling to their holes. If some very modern-minded person here, fed up with old phrases like "original sin," wants to call it *Id* instead, you are quite welcome. But you do not by that escape man's deep and tragic need—salvation from something inherently wrong with him. As another put it: "To expect a change in human nature may be an act of faith, but to expect a change in human society without it is an act of lunacy."

That is where we stand today, confronting man's folly and wickedness. And yet, there is the New Testament! Something else true about man! Something else in us profounder than our sinfulness! As St. Augustine, with all his stress on human depravity, put it long ago: "Dig deep enough in any man and you will find something divine." Do we really believe that about ourselves?

First of all, note that this emphasis, with which the New Testament is radiant, goes back to Jesus and his way of dealing with individual men and women. Jesus was no sentimentalist about man. He could blaze with indignation against human evil. He said that some men deserved to have stones hung about their necks and to be cast into the depths of the sea. He knew the sin of man. Did it not spit on him, crown him with thorns and crucify him? But always beneath his realistic appraisal of man's depravity was his faith in man, something divine there if one could only get at it, appeal to it, open the way for God's grace to release it.

He faced a woman taken in adultery, dragged before him as a guilty sinner, condemned by the law to be stoned. But when her accusers had retreated, and Jesus was left alone with her, he drove home his appeal to something in her deeper than her sinfulness, something which her accusers did not believe was there, but which he knew must be there, until he reached it—how we wish we knew the whole conversation he had with that woman!—so that he could say to her in parting, "Neither do I condemn thee. Go. Sin no more." Beneath our worst Jesus never doubted the presence of that inner light that "lighteth every man."

Well, is not that the deepest fact about us? We are sinners, but then we know we are. There is the mystery. A pig is a pig, but he does not know it. I am a sinner, but I know it. There is a judgment seat inside me, a divine voice within me distinguishing right from wrong, condemning my evil, a light that makes my darkness visible. That is the profoundest fact about us. One of our modern skeptics calls man "an ingenious assembly of portable plumbing." To be sure, that is part of us, but that isn't what we are. We *have* an ingenious assembly of portable plumbing, but we *are* souls with hours when "the spirit's true endowments stand out plainly from the false ones." We are souls in which, if you dig deep enough, you will find something divine. Say your worst about us, Wordsworth is still right:

> There's not a man
> That lives, who hath not known
>   his godlike hours.

That is the mystery of man, and to face thus what we really are can be the most determining moment in a man's life.

Remember Jesus' description of the prodigal son in the far country that day when he made his great decision: "When he came to himself," said Jesus; "when he came to himself he said . . . I will arise and go to my father." Something in himself which did not belong in the far country! Something in himself not at home among swine! He had asked his father for his inheritance, and had thought he had been given it in money, but now he awoke to the fact that his heritage went deeper— an inheritance of the spirit without which he was not himself at all. When he came to himself, his real self, he arose. That was Jesus' undiscourageable insight into human nature.

Recall that day when to Simon, vacillating, impulsive, unsteady, unreliable, Simon, Jesus said, "Thou art Peter . . . rock." Not first of all you ought to be rock, but you are rock; that is the deepest fact about you, underneath all your failure, rock on which the very church of Christ could be built.

To someone here today the Master is trying to say something like that. Who do you think you really are? A bit of organic scum, or a son of God—what a difference! Remember King Lear: "Who is it that can tell me who I am? I would learn that." Christianity's answer to that question is clear. We are potential sons of God, and as Nietzsche said, although alas! he never lived up to it, "Become what you really are."

Let us go on now to a second fact. This emphasis in the New Testament on man's dignity, value and divine possibility goes back not only to Jesus' attitude toward others, but to what he was himself. Constantly in the church we stress the doctrine that Christ was the revelation of God. To be sure he was! But today let us face another aspect of Christian doctrine—Christ was also the revelation of man. He became man; he shared our human nature. So that is what manhood and womanhood at their best are—Christlike. Even Pilate when he led the thorn-crowned Master out before the raging crowd cried, "Behold! the man!"

If I could make that truth, that Christ is the revelation not only of God but of man, real to myself and to you today, it would meet a deep need in all of us. For the newspapers flood us daily with tales of filth, corruption, meanness, depravity, so that we find ourselves saying, That is human nature. From pictures of human conduct in Kinsey reports and rotten novels to actual human conduct that anyone can see, from dirty politics to the horrors of modern war, we are faced with the crassness and coarseness of man. And now comes the New Testament, crying for all the world to hear that Christ is man; and what is more, as one of the early church fathers put it, "Christ became what we are that we might become what he is." The New Testament is full of that. "Until we all attain," it says, "to mature manhood, to the measure of the stature of the fullness of Christ." "But we all," it cries, "with unveiled face beholding . . . the glory of the Lord, are transformed into the same image from glory to glory." Does that at first seem to someone here downright incredible? I agree! I tell you it is much easier to believe in the Christian idea of God than in the Christian idea of man.

Nevertheless, here is the stark fact. Long ago that man appeared with nothing but his character, what he was in himself, to impress the race—a character so much too good for this naughty world that few believed in him and the powers that be crucified him—and yet now some two thousand years afterwards we are celebrating, not Pilate, not Judas, not the scoundrels who hated him, and the blind minds who could not love the highest when they saw him, but Christ! There is something in us that responds to him, that makes the centuries respond to him, that has issued in multitudes of Christlike lives who have illumined history. Dig deep enough in man, and you will find something divine.

Let us take this truth home to ourselves! Christian living is commonly presented as a beautiful, far-off ideal. We ought to be thus and so; we ought to be Christlike; we ought; we ought! That's all true, but the Bible strikes a deeper note. We are. We are made in the image of God. At our deepest that is what we are. To be Christlike is to be oneself fulfilled. You are not a weed, Christianity says, trying to be a oak tree; you are an oak. Then become what you really are! You cannot do it by yourself alone. An oak tree needs cosmic backing—air, sunlight, rain— so you need the grace of God. But you are not a weed; you are an oak. That is the Christian gospel.

Gutzon Borglum, the sculptor, was once working on a head of Abraham Lincoln. Each day he chipped away the stone, and each day it was the task of a Negro woman to sweep up the pieces and carry them off. Amazed, she watched the head of Lincoln emerge under the sculptor's hands until at last, when the work was almost finished, she could hold in her wonder no longer. "Mr. Borglum," she said. "How'd you know Mr. Lincoln was in dat stone?" Well, the emergence of great character from the rough rock of our unshaped lives often seems utterly improbable, but Christian faith has been insistent: Mr. Lincoln is in that stone!

This then is the practical consequence of the matter: identify yourself today with your best self, not with your worst. The worst is there; you know it all too well, but never call that your true self. You have potential Christlikeness in you; it is there. I have seen lives transfigured by the recognition of that fact. They have been identifying themselves with their worst, so that they thought themselves peanuts, bits of organic scum, hopeless sinners. Then the new insight came, like John Keats picking up Spenser's *Faerie Queene*, and as he read it seeing what he really was—a poet! I am a poet! So I have seen lives made over by insight into what they really are. That could happen here today.

I know that sudden conversion is not often talked about in these days. It sounds very old-fashioned. But some time since reading a book on psychology, I ran on the phrase: "instantaneous reorientation." Can you beat it? That psychologist would never have condescended to say, sudden conversion, but "instantaneous reorientation," *that* is all right. He has seen that happen. So have I. Call it what you will, it could happen here now. "When he came to himself he said . . . I will arise."

As for the world at large, how desperately we need this message! The world is a mess. Yet let an old man say a final word to you young people here about this chaotic, frightening generation. No swift solution is in sight. Don't expect it! We are in for a long, hard haul. But this is not the first time in history that mankind has faced a dismaying era. In 1848 Lord Shaftsbury said, "Nothing can save the British Empire from shipwreck." In 1849 Disraeli said, "In industry, commerce and agriculture there is no hope." In 1852 the dying Duke of Wellington said, "I thank God I shall be spared from seeing the consummation of ruin that is gathering about us." Nevertheless, don't tell me that all these years since have been only wasted motion, getting us nowhere. Doors of opportunity are open to us that were not here when I was born. The gifts of science can be turned to peaceful purposes; the new world-wide proximity which has brought friction and hostility can be transformed into neighborliness. God is not dead, and, as for man, don't read the newspaper headlines only, read the New Testament too! The future belongs not to Pilate—Oh, never to Pilate!—but to the Master, and the kingdom of this world can become the kingdom of our Lord and of his Christ.

Who Killed Jesus?[1]

O NCE in Palestine I climbed the slope of the Mount of Olives to look across the Kidron Valley into Jerusalem. From Olivet one can see the whole circle of the city's walls and on the nearer side the great stone platform where, in the Master's day, stood Herod's new and shining temple. Could one have been there that first Palm Sunday morning, he could have seen the little company come around the brow of the hill from Bethany and dip down into the Kidron Valley, thence to climb to the gates amid the waving of palm branches and the cry of "Hosanna to the son of David." A few days later, had he been there, he might have seen three crosses lifted north of the city's wall, and might have watched them through the day until they were silhouetted against the darkening evening sky. There is no place in the world, I think, more fertile in meditation than the Mount of Olives during Holy Week.

This morning I invite you there to look down upon Jerusalem and inquire, Who killed Jesus? When any dramatic meeting of good and evil has passed into history, been clothed in imagination, sung in poetry, painted in art, one thing always happens: we become vehement partisans of one side against the other, see our heroes very bright and their enemies very black. So, in our childhood, William Tell and all the Swiss were angels to us and

[1] A Palm Sunday sermon.

the Hapsburgs demons. So William Wallace and Robert Bruce were saints and the English under Edward I were devils. This contrast between black and white has been the inevitable color scheme of the crucifixion as Christians have looked back upon it. Here was the Saviour, fairest among ten thousand and the one altogether lovely, and there were cruel and knavish men who despised him and slew him between thieves. The cross of Christ is so terrible that one naturally thinks of the men who were responsible for it as abysmal brutes. Because, however, I feel sure this was not true, I ask this morning, Who killed Jesus?

One of the most solemnizing facts about the crucifixion is that the men who sent Jesus to his cross were ordinary people and that the motives which moved them were among the most familiar that play upon our lives today. I almost dread trying to make that as real to you as it seems to me, for there is no hiding for our consciences when the picture is complete. The people of Jerusalem were very ordinary folk and the motives that persuaded them to the crucifixion among the most familiar that operate today.

To be sure, we would not crucify Jesus. We have grown more tender about pain since then. We would not lift three crosses upon Calvary.

> When Jesus came to Golgotha they hanged
>   Him on a tree,
> They drave great nails through hands and
>   feet, and made a Calvary;
> They crowned Him with a crown of thorns,
>   red were His wounds and deep,
> For those were crude and cruel days, and
>   human flesh was cheap.

When Jesus came to Birmingham they simply
    passed Him by,
They never hurt a hair of Him, they only
    let Him die;
For men had grown more tender, and they
    would not give Him pain,
They only just passed down the street, and
    left Him in the rain.

Still Jesus cried, "Forgive them, for they
    know not what they do,"
And still it rained the winter rain that
    drenched Him through and through;
The crowds went home and left the streets
    without a soul to see,
And Jesus crouched against a wall and
    cried for Calvary.[2]

Just so! Who, then, killed Jesus?

In the first place, religious people in whom religion had
hardened into stiff and formal shapes. So far from being bad
folk, they were among the best of their time. To be sure, the
Gospels give an unlovely portrait of the Pharisees, for they had
the faults of their qualities which stood out against the ministry
of Jesus, but there is another side to their characters. In the old
days, when the Greeks under Antiochus Epiphanes crashed
down upon Jerusalem, violated the temple, sacrificed swine upon
the altar and tore to pieces the rolls of the sacred Law, the
Pharisees rose up for the protection of their desecrated faith.
Their name, Pharisee, means Puritan, and like our Puritans

[2] "Indifference" from *The Unutterable Beauty* by G. A. Studdert-
Kennedy, used by permission of Harper & Brothers.

they had a long tradition of courageous resistance. They had saved Judaism. And now that Greece had gone and Rome had come, with its overwhelming power and its terrible seductiveness for Jewish youth, they still were saving Judaism. They believed in God; they believed in his revelation to Israel; they saw that they had a higher standard of monotheistic faith and practical morality than the heathenism that was pressing in upon them; they believed that their Law was an entrustment from on high, and they had dedicated their lives to building a dyke to protect their people from the encroaching sea of pagan faith and morals. They were not bad folk. They were among the best folk of their time.

But how could they endure Jesus? Of course, he believed in God, but they caught the drift of his words and saw that if his ideas were allowed free course there soon would come a perilously broad idea of God that would overflow their safeguards and take in Jew and Gentile, barbarian, Scythian, bond and free. To be sure, he believed in righteousness—one could see that—but how could that comfort them when he would not accept their definitions of righteousness and even dared to say, "It was said to them of old time . . . but I say unto you." Of course, he believed in the Scriptures but, then, he picked and chose what he wanted there, and as for precise laws of sabbatic observance or requirements about clean and unclean foods, he threw them altogether away. Of course, he was a good man but, then, he was so lax about sinners; he so let down the fences for them; he even loved them and seemed to think returning prodigals his special care. Obviously, they could not tolerate Jesus or endure with equanimity the scene on Palm Sunday morning with throngs around him crying, "Hosanna to the Son of David."

Who, then, killed Jesus? These men killed him, respectable people, conscientious people in whom religion had stiffened into hard forms. Have you ever seen a river choked by its own ice? That is the perennial truth about religion. It is living water, without which no man can live well, but it freezes into hard forms of organization, creed, ritual and custom and then the free-flowing stream is blocked by its own congealing. That has happened in Buddhism, in Confucianism, in Islam, in Judaism, and in Christianity. It always has happened. It is happening today. It happened in ancient Jerusalem. And it killed Jesus.

I stood on Olivet trying to be angry with the ancient Pharisees for what they had done to our Lord, but I found myself praying instead: God have mercy on our organized religion for what we today are doing to him still!

It was not, however, organized religion only but organized business that put the Master to death. His cross was partly due to businessmen who had found how very pleasant big profits feel. They, too, were not bad men. They had no desire to hurt Jesus. Listen to them argue! If Jesus had minded his own business and left them alone they would have been most glad to mind their business and leave him alone. They were the last people to desire trouble and publicity. They were profitably engaged in trade in the temple courts according to the current standards of the time. If a pilgrim came to Jerusalem, why should he not have to change his foreign currency into temple money, and why should not the money-changers, in the courts, who, after all, had only a seasonal occupation when the big pilgrimages were on, charge a fat fee for the exchange? Anyway, the poor money-changers had to send a large rake-off to the high priest's office for the privilege of being there at all. Moreover, if a pilgrim wanted to offer a sheep upon the altar, why should not the temple traders stand in with the official censors, so that a sheep bought in the cheap markets of the city always had a blemish on it and only the sheep bought at high prices in the temple courts managed to get by? Business is business.

Here in New York City a friend of mine called upon a merchant known to be a professing Christian and a member of the church, who made him a frankly unethical proposition. My friend said, "I am surprised that a man like you, known to be a church member, should make me such a proposition." "Why!" said the merchant in surprise, "Do you mean to say that you mix your religion and your business and so spoil both?" On that principle they were working in the temple courts. Moreover, those money-changers had families to support, and what more sacred obligation rests on anybody than to support one's family? They were not bad folk. They were among the friendliest, kindest, most courteous and urbane people in Jerusalem. Only, obviously, they could not endure Jesus. The crucifixion of Jesus had not been determined on until the day when he cleansed the temple courts, overturned the tables of the money-changers and with his whip of cords drove out the sheep. Up to that point even the religious people had not decided on his death. But that settled it. He had touched Jerusalem on a most sensitive nerve— profits. Businessmen of the city rose up in wrath to say that such unwarranted interference with current methods of trade was not to be tolerated.

That is not ancient history. I have been frank about the unchristian aspects of that area of life where I habitually work— organized religion. Will you be equally frank about the unchristian aspects of that area of life where many of you work?

Here in New York, a few years before the Civil War, a New

York merchant called out from an antislavery meeting Mr. May, a prominent philanthropist, and spoke to him as follows:

Mr. May, we are not such fools as not to know that slavery is a great evil; a great wrong. But it was consented to by the founders of our Republic. It was provided for in the Constitution of our Union. A great portion of the property of the Southerners is invested under its sanction; and the business of the North, as well as the South, has become adjusted to it. There are millions upon millions of dollars due from Southerners to the merchants and mechanics of this city alone, the payment of which would be jeopardized by any rupture between the North and the South. We cannot afford, sir, to let you and your associates succeed in your endeavor to overthrow slavery. It is not a matter of principle with us. It is a matter of business necessity. We cannot afford to let you succeed. I have called you out to let you know, and to let your fellow-laborers know, that we do not mean to allow you to succeed. We mean sir [he said with increased emphasis—] we mean, sir, to put you Abolitionists down— by fair means if we can, by foul means if we must.

Any man who knows history knows how familiar that tone of voice is wherever, in any generation, profits have been touched. I sat on Olivet remembering angrily those old businessmen in Jerusalem who did our Lord to death, until I recalled that one of the most thoughtful economists of America said, "The master iniquities of our time are connected with money-making." How continuously, with the same old motives, we crucify Christ still!

Not simply organized religion and organized business, organized politics also helped to raise the cross. Politicians doing what politicians commonly do—playing safe—killed Jesus. Even Pilate was not very bad. He did not wish to harm Jesus. He tried every corner that he could turn to avoid it. "I find no fault in this man," he kept saying, and being a Roman with an ingrained

desire to do justice if he could, he did not relish putting to death
anyone in whom he found no fault. But what could Pilate do?
Caiaphas, the Sadducee, and his associates were wily, shrewd
politicians, more than Pilate's match. They saw clearly and, I
suspect, thought honestly that Jesus was claiming to be the Messiah, that such a claim would probably mean public uproar,
perhaps revolution, that this would mean a Roman army, in-
demnities, limited liberties, and perhaps bloodshed. Caiaphas
surveyed the situation with the cool, keen, analyzing eye of the
expert politician. He saw that probably they would have to do
one of two things, neither of which was ideal. "It is expedient,"
he said, using the politican's favorite word, "it is expedient for
you that one man should die for the people, and that the whole
nation perish not." As for Pilate, he could not afford to be
accused of laxness in forestalling a popular uprising. He could
not politically afford to be suspected of looseness in his loyalty
to Caesar. That crowd out there, yelling at him, had been well
instructed what to say. "Away with him. . . . We have no
king but Caesar." Obviously Pilate, as a good politician, had to
play safe.

Anatole France wrote a story in which he represented Pilate
and a friend of his long years afterward talking about Palestine
and their experiences there, from the strange characters they had
met and the dancing girls they had known, to the tumultuous
history in which they had played a part. Then Pilate's friend
casually asked him whether he remembered Jesus of Nazareth,
who had been crucified. Pilate knit his brows in vain. "Jesus,"
he murmured, "Jesus of Nazareth? I cannot call him to mind."
That day's work was a forgotten incident in the political game.

My friends, it is a devastating experience to sit on Olivet and
see how easy and natural it all was down there in Jerusalem.

When have popular politicians stopped playing safe? We are more suave now. We would not nail men to crosses, but anybody can see that there is no motive in Caiaphas or Pilate that is not the common property of popular politics today. Playing safe, doing what the crowd cries to have done, even when the man knows it should not be done—that is familiar. But it was that which crucified Jesus.

It is incredible, someone protests, that so terrible a thing as the crucifixion of Jesus should have been caused by the familiar motives running through our organized religion, organized business, and organized politics today; there must be something dark and damnable behind the crucifixion of Jesus, something cruel, knavish and sinister, to which we can stand superior, on which we can look down and vent our indignation as lovers of the Lord who shrink from his murderers as from a pestilence. If you feel like that, of whom are you thinking? Of Herod, of Judas, of the Roman soldiers? Look at them!

Herod was a typical man of the world. You would have found him, I suspect, quite debonair, witty, worldly-wise, and a regular good fellow. Of course, he had no moral scruples. He fell in love with his brother's wife and took her. Why not? He wanted her and he got away with it. Moreover, if he loved her and she loved him, why were they not justified in making two lives happy at the expense of one life's unhappiness? That is a familiar argument. I heard it this last week from one of the participants. As for responsibility for Jesus' death, that was Pilate's business, not his. So he sent Jesus back to Pilate and, I presume, promptly forgot the matter, told another good story to his boon companions, and took another drink. That is a familiar type. There are many Herods in New York today.

As for Judas, O disciple of Jesus, beware how you think of him as uniquely bad! He was so intensely interested in the Kingdom of God that in days when it was dangerous and unpopular he joined the circle of Jesus' followers. He gave up his business; he gave up his home; he became a wandering follower of the new prophet. He had stuff in him. Yes, and after his base betrayal began to bring its fatal fruit and he saw the looming of the cruel cross, he walked up like a man to the Sanhedrin, from the very outskirts of which Peter had fled, and, saying, "I have betrayed innocent blood," he threw down his ill-gotten money, and went out and hanged himself for shame He had a conscience. Only, he had begun to lose faith in Jesus. He had watched this strange program of a peaceable and gentle Messiah, so different from what he had expected. Where, then, was that real Messiah who would rule the Gentiles with a rod of iron and dash them to pieces like a potter's vessel? He had lost faith in Jesus. Disillusionment had settled on him. He was angry at being so deceived about the Messiah. He thought he would reimburse himself: some pay—was it not justified for all the sacrifice that he had made for this pale, milk-and-water, enfeebled counterfeit of a world saviour who would talk nothing but love? Lost faith, disillusionment, resurgent selfishness—that is Judas. Anything strange about it? "He that is without sin among you, let him first cast a stone."

If you say that the Roman soldiers were especially cruel and wicked, what do you mean? Crucifixion was part of their business. They were paid to do that. Shall a man not earn his wages? As for the soldiers' mockery of Jesus, since when has Jew-baiting ceased to be a Gentile prerogative? Moreover, it is a soldier's business always to do stern, cruel things when he is commanded to. We have grown used, even in these years of our Lord, under the aegis of official sanction from the Church of Christ, to see soldiers sent out to screw bayonets into the abdomens of their enemies as a holy duty, to drop bombs on mothers and children in their villages as a sacred obligation, to blow up ships at sea as a dedicated task? The Roman soldiers were not specially bad. They did their work, I take it, as gently as they could.

My friends, where shall we hide our souls? There was not a motive in Jerusalem that last week when Christ was so disowned and crucified that is not in ourselves. Even the crowd! Oh, especially the crowd! That was the final element in the crucifixion of Jesus and it was a typical specimen of mob psychology. Somebody who understood well how to handle the matter set a few people crying, "Crucify him," and soon the crowd had caught it up and it was rising like the surges of the sea. Watch these men go down David Street that morning with no idea of what is afoot. Obviously something is afoot; a crowd has gathered. Were you ever able to pass a street crowd without stopping to see what was doing? So they stop and listen as once more the growing throng lifts up its hoarse and raucous cry, "Release Barabbas but crucify *him*." "What is it all about?" says one. "Jesus of Galilee," comes the answer, "bound to get us into trouble with the Romans unless we can be rid of him." Well, it is obvious, is it not, that Jerusalem cannot afford to have any more trouble with the Romans? So one more voice joins the throng and then another, relishing, as we all do, the sense of unanimity with the multitude, loving to cry one thing with a crowd, although not understanding what it is about—"Crucify him, crucify him!" I thought I heard the echoes upon Olivet. Alas, it was so easy to get rid of Jesus!

Yet, after all these centuries the world is not rid of him. There were a few people in Jerusalem who would not help to crucify

him. Nicodemus, the rabbi, a man of religion, Joseph of Ari-
mathaea, a man of business and a member of the political coun-
cil, a little group of disciples who passionately adored him, a
few women who stood afar off from the cross and wept—so small
a bridge they seemed for him to cross to his world triumph, but
he crossed it. When, in George Bernard Shaw's play, they tell
Joan of Arc that they are going to burn her at the stake, she
foresees the effect upon the people. "If I go through the fire,"
she says, "I shall go through it to their hearts for ever and ever."
So he moves, though slowly, to his triumph. But God have
mercy upon some of us for what we are doing to him yet!

A Religion to Support Democracy[1]

IN the generation in which some of us were reared, we assumed that as knowledge increased and progress continued mankind would, of course, accept ever more universally the democratic faith and practice. Instead, democracy stands now in critical peril and we are celebrating Lincoln's birthday under circumstances that lend peculiar poignancy to his desire that "a government of the people, by the people, for the people" should not perish from the earth.

With this situation we, as Christians, are vitally concerned. There is an essential relationship between the individual Christian conscience before God, on one side, and, on the other, civil liberties, the Bill of Rights, and the freedom of minorities under democratic rule. Say as we will that Christians can manage to be Christian under any kind of government, still they are having a desperate time of it in Russia. Democracy has done for us as Christians an incalculable service, and now in her hour of need democracy asks us what we can do for her. What kind of religion ought ours to be if it is to support the democratic faith and practice?

As we face this theme, one fact towers high. Democracy cannot be merely inherited. It must be reborn with every generation. Dictatorship can, in a way, be inherited; it rests upon coercion,

[1] A Lincoln's Birthday sermon.

and a tyrant, if he be skillful and powerful enough, can hand on to his successor the regime he has by force established, as has been done in many a dynasty. But democracy is spiritually engendered in the hearts of its individual citizens. It depends on qualities of personal character, the responsible use of freedom, the willingness to hear and weigh contrary opinions debated in the state, inner devotion to the public good that makes outer coercion needless, voluntary performance of the duties democracy entails. So the democratic faith and spirit, depending on qualities that cannot be coerced, must be reborn in each generation. Unless the inner spiritual factors that created democracy in the first place can thus be constantly renewed, its outward forms fall into decay.

Here have been our fault and our apostasy. We have taken democracy for granted. We have thought our fathers created it and handed it down to us and that we accepted it. Now, however, it is clear that if we are to preserve democracy we must ourselves recover the creative spiritual factors that originally produced it. The first line of democratic defense is not against an external foe but against an internal loss of those ideas and qualities that must in every generation reproduce democracy.

Today I share with you a strong conviction that these ideas and qualities are impregnated with a religious character, that they are in their source and sustenance spiritual, and that few questions are as important as this: What kind of religion ought ours to be if it is to support a government of, by and for the people?

In the first place, obviously it must be a religion that dignifies personality. Democracy springs from a high estimate of persons. At the heart of democracy is not so much a political process as a spiritual faith that values and trusts persons. Said Thomas Jefferson: "The care of human life and happiness, and not their destruction, is the first and only legitimate object of good government." We take that for granted but at first it was new, like the discovery of Copernicus that reoriented the solar system. Democracy lifted a revolutionary idea that persons are central in importance, that they do not exist for the sake of the state but that the state exists for the sake of them.

Moreover, democracy not only values but trusts persons with an amazing faith whose validity has yet to be proved, trusts people with freedom to think, to say what they think, to hear all sides of public questions discussed, to balance opposing arguments and to decide. That is an astonishing confidence in people. The dictators would say that it is an insane confidence. There are few articles of the Nicene Creed which require more downright faith than that. The founding fathers themselves were not unanimous about it. Said Alexander Hamilton, "The people is a great beast." Yet faith in people is the soul of democracy.

Nowhere is the contrast between democracy and dictatorship more evident than here. Dictatorship says that persons exist primarily for the sake of the state; democracy says that the state exists primarily for the sake of persons. Dictatorship herds persons like sheep, hypnotizes them by mass propaganda, coerces them by mass pressure; democracy trusts persons as the ultimate sources of decision in the commonwealth. As between these two estimates of personality, the one democratic and the other dictatorial, there is no question, is there, where the genius and spirit of Christ's teachings stand? When Jesus said, "It is not the will of your Father . . . that one of these little ones should perish," when he pled for the one lost sheep, lost coin, lost son, when he said about even the most sacred institutions of his people, "The sabbath was made for man, and not man for the sabbath," when from every angle of approach he moved up to personality as supremely valuable, loved of God and capable of being God's child, he was not simply laying the foundations of a new religion, he was laying the foundations of Western democracy. For our democracy has sprung from two main sources: early Greek experiments with popular government and Christ's emphasis on the worth of persons. That is where democracy came from in the first place. There its strength must forever be renewed.

Materialistic irreligion denies this estimate. It reduces the human being to an accidental collocation of physical atoms. Carried to its logical conclusion, it makes people what another calls "impotent nobodies hurtling toward nothingness." We cannot build a successful democracy on that idea. Some of us can recall when first this doctrine of materialistic irreligion came up over our horizon. How roused and shocked we were as Christians! This idea, we said, will destroy the church. But today we see a further truth. I wish it could be shouted from the housetops: this devaluation of persons will destroy democracy.

This last week I stepped into the office of one of the leading exponents of scientific medicine in this city. "What do you think of the world?" he said. "It is in a sorry state," I answered. "Yes," he replied, and then, as though he were the preacher and I the layman, he added, "It will be in a sorry state as long as we think there is nothing more to the human mind and spirit than two physical cells that accidentally got together."

If there is no more in persons than materialism sees, why should we trust them to think, to hear all sides of great questions and to decide? Why should we commit to such creatures' collective judgment the destiny of nations? What right have such physical automata to the sacred privileges of intellectual and spiritual freedom? In the name of democracy I plead on Lincoln's birthday for a return to a Christian philosophy of life and a Christian estimate of the worth of persons—not accidents of the coagulated dust, but sons and daughters of God with possibilities that only the eternal ages can reveal, not, therefore, merely existing for the sake of the state, but the state and every other human institution existing for them. Never can we achieve a successful democracy on a slighter faith than that.

In the second place, the kind of religion that will support government of, by and for the people is one that recognizes a higher loyalty than the state. Let a man stand back from the democratic process and look at it as though he saw it for the first time and how easy it is to understand why dictators deride it! For we set up a government to rule a nation and then deliberately introduce opposition parties and minorities to hector the government, criticize it and obstruct its policies. That seems to a dictator a weird idea. Yet behind it is an essential democratic faith that there is something higher than any government, to which our primary allegiance belongs. You are not the slaves of government, says democracy; think for yourselves, if need be differ from the government and oppose it; there is a higher loyalty than the government to which you must be true. It is as though democracy, with its doctrine of minorities, essentially were saying, We must obey God rather than man.

All too common is the idea that the essence of democracy is the rule of the majority. That is not true. Dictatorship also can be and often is the rule of the majority. Would not even a free election in Russia bring a majority for the dictator? Russia too may claim to be under the rule of the majority. But the unique distinction of democracy Russia utterly lacks—not the rule of the majority, but the rights of the minorities. There lies the peculiar quality of the democratic idea.

That idea is not to be taken easily for granted. The possibility and validity of the idea have yet to be proved, and if we here in America cannot make a success of it, then I suspect it is doomed. See how crazy it can be made to appear! We set up a government and then actually pay salaries to opposition party members in the legislatures to criticize and obstruct the government. Looked at in cold logicality, that is an insane idea! Yes, but it is magnificent too, one of the greatest political faiths ever ventured on in all history. The British have a phrase that in these days moves me deeply: "His Majesty's Most Loyal Opposition." That is democracy and it is magnificent.

It takes real faith, even in this country, to support this democratic idea in our time. For communists play a clever game, working temporarily within the democratic system, praising democracy, using democratic slogans, whereas everybody knows that, were they to win, they would kick out from under them the ladder of freedom by which they climbed and destroy the very Bill of Rights they temporarily made use of. Moreover, in opposition, fascist minds arise, impatient with this turmoil of minority opinions. We cannot sail the ship of state, they cry, by a weather vane, and this democratic clash of opinion is like a medley of winds blowing from all directions; give us somebody's strong and settled will from whose arbitrament there is no appeal.

Even in this country it is not easy to hold hard by the democratic idea. Yet though the rights of minorities be abused and though the impatience of dictatorial minds be understandable, still the democratic faith remains the best hope of mankind, and

without it—I measure my words—Christianity may not survive.
For to the Christian no human government can ever be the
highest loyalty. The rights of minorities were, as a matter of
history, created in the first place by the religious conscience obey-
ing God rather than men. There, in a religious idea, this element
of democracy was first produced and there it must find its perennial renewal. Here, too, the church can help to kindle the
faith that supports the democratic system and, what it claims for
itself, can contend for on behalf of others, whether agreeing
with them or not—a loyalty that surpasses the state, the right to
be, "His Majesty's Most Loyal Opposition." For the Christian
conscience and civil liberties are done up in one bundle of life.

In the third place, the kind of religion that will support the
democratic faith and practice must genuinely care not only for
the liberty but for the equality and fraternity of the people. Our
attention in these days is concentrated on the external enemies
of democracy, the dictatorships that threaten war. It would be
insane to minimize that peril. But the deeper danger to democracy is still within. It lies in the inequalities among our own
people that spoil fraternity, destroy loyalty, divide us into economic classes, and make real democracy impossible.

Let no one try an easy escape from this by laughing off the
phrase in the Declaration of Independence about all men being
created equal. The founding fathers did not think that all men
have the same I. Q. They did mean, however, that equality of
right, of opportunity, and of general economic condition underlay the hope of a free nation. When De Toqueville visited this
country in its early days, he said, "Amongst the novel objects
that attracted my attention during my stay in the United States,
nothing struck me more forcibly than the general equality of

condition among the people." So political democracy was born out of economic democracy, when there was a general equality of condition among the people. Recall how Daniel Webster put it in 1820: "With property divided, as we have it, no other government than that of a republic could be maintained, even were we foolish enough to desire it." So, it was a general economic equality that made political democracy inevitable.

Then, only a little more than a century after Webster's remark, one listens to the Brookings Institution reporting on incomes of American families: "Thus it appears that one-tenth of one per cent of the families at the top received practically as much as forty-two per cent of the families at the bottom of the scale." That bodes ill to the republic.

This does not mean that the people in the one-tenth of one per cent at the economic top are the enemies of democracy and the people in the forty-two per cent are its friends. Upon the contrary, one finds among the one-tenth of one per cent some of the most intelligent friends of democracy and among the forty-two per cent one sometimes finds crazy movements that make straight for the totalitarian state. This is not a matter for personal blame; it is far too serious for class recrimination; it is the situation itself, in which both sides are caught, that is perilous.

Would not Jesus say that? For here, too, one runs headlong into the essential kinship between democracy and Christ. The dignifying of personality—there they are at one. A higher loyalty for conscience than the state—there they are at one. The peril to mankind of the rich over against the poor, Dives on the one side, Lazarus lying at the gate upon the other—there they are at one. With what constant emphasis Jesus bore down on that—the peril of economic privilege to the soul of the possessor, the peril of economic inequality to the brotherhood of man.

In our time, the danger in this situation, so far as democracy is concerned, has become acute because it is on this that communism feeds; it is the alleviation and cure of this that communism promises; it is because of this that communism spreads. The way in which communism proposes to solve the problem, however, runs all against the democratic grain. Communism proposes the state ownership and conduct of economic processes. That means that the two most powerful coercive forces in the world, the political and economic, would be concentrated in the same hands. Now, when the political and economic powers are thus concentered in the same hands, no nation can stop there. The nation must go on, as communism has gone on in Russia, to destroy opposing parties and minorities, deny the dangerous liberty of speech and press that might impede the smooth running of the regimented system on which now the people's subsistence hangs, must go on to solidify under mass control the thinking and action of the people. When we centralize in the same hands these two most powerful coercive forces in the world, be sure that our civil liberties will soon be gone. The price is too high for what is promised. Recall the saying of Chateaubriand about his temptation to easygoing solutions, "agreeing," he said, "to a century of bondage to avoid an hour's fuss." Well, we must decline communism's century of bondage to save ourselves from an hour's fuss.

All the more, however, as Christians and as believers in democracy, we must face the fact that ultimately there is no possibility of a successful political democracy without economic democracy. If we cannot achieve that end by communism's way, then we must find a democratic way of achieving it. Let any Christianity that would sustain democracy see and say this in the name of the Christ, at the very heart of whose teaching lies the principle on which the fact rests. So long ago it was said in England, "That which makes a few rich and many poor suits not the commonwealth."

Finally, the kind of religion that will support government of, by and for the people must create responsible personal character in the individual citizens. Our American scene lamentably displays the lack of this. We commonly praise freedom as the essence of democracy. Our fathers won liberty for us and this gift we have inherited—so runs popular thinking—and all the time the solemn, yes tragic, aspect of the matter goes forgotten, that freedom is a curse when not accompanied and balanced by intelligent, responsible personal character. What do we mean by so centering all attention on freedom? There are some people we dare not set free. It is worse than throwing dynamite about. It is dangerous to set criminals free. It is dangerous to set morons and imbeciles free. It is dangerous to set free too many irresponsible egoists, motived by greed, who think all of themselves and nothing of the common good. That spells ruin. Too many people in our republic, high and low, clamor for freedom with no sense of responsibility for its public-spirited use. A chastened stress on liberty and more stress on responsibility befits us well. For freedom has an indispensable correlative: namely, responsible, public-spirited personal character.

Put it this way. A great population must be controlled. No sentimentality should blind our eyes to that realistic fact. If there is to be order and not chaos, discipline not anarchy, people must be controlled. And there are only two ways of controlling them.

Coercion from without—that is one. Voluntary, responsible, public-spirited character spiritually engendered within—that is the other. A dictatorship stakes its very existence on the method of coercion, while a democracy remains a democracy only in so far as voluntary, responsible, public-spirited character takes coercion's place. In any nation, the more we have of one, the less we have of the other. If we have a growing ascendancy of coercion, as, alas! is true in this country now, be sure it is because the responsible initiative of personal character is failing. If we have less and less necessity of coercion, be sure it is because the responsible initiative of personal character is growing. Is not this the very crux of the matter in America? We cannot go on forever in the republic neglecting those character-building faiths and incentives from which personal quality and moral integrity spring.

Here, too, Christ and democracy are at one. Whatever else Christianity at its best has done, it has produced self-starting, self-motivating, self-driving character. Church of Christ, this day of crisis and alarm is also the day of your opportunity if democracy is to be saved. A republic must be built, not on coercion but on voluntary, inwardly right, responsible, personal character, to produce which should be your specialty. And you who have been careless of religion, negligent of the church, thoughtless of Christ, in general separate from the character-building faiths of mankind, but who do care about government of, by and for the people, have we not a right to appeal to you to rethink your attitude?

Some tell us that the devotion of Russian youth to the Kremlin is thrilling and that we in America have nothing to match it. I wish we could feel an equal thrill born of an equal devotion to democracy and to the kind of religion that sustains it. The dignifying of personality, the giving of conscience to God above all human institutions, the achievement not of popular liberty alone but of popular equality and fraternity, the erection of human society on transformed, inwardly regenerate, responsible personal character—that is the cause on which the highest hopes of mankind depend. There is the cause that on Lincoln's birthday should stir the imagination and elicit the loyalty of us all.

The Temptations of Maturity

THIS generation has been emphatically concerned about child-hood. To be sure, before our day a Roman priest remarked that, if the Church can have a child until he is seven years old, it matters not who has him afterwards. In our time, however, the new psychology, tracing the formative influences of character back into the early years of infancy, has created the impression in many people that life's problem is practically solved if the child has a good start.

Indeed, whoever has seen a life stepped on when it was young and has watched the consequence, can never underestimate the importance of a fine beginning. Nevertheless, you must have friends like some that I have had. They were not stepped on when they were young. They did have a fine beginning. They came out of a promising youth, fulfilled the expectations of their friends, rose to positions of distinguished trust, and then, on the crest of their career, went all to pieces.

Thinking of such life histories, one remembers the arresting words of Jesus: "This man began to build, and was not able to finish." This morning, as you see, dealing with the temptations and moral collapses of maturity, I am speaking to my own genera-tion. You young people, habitually addressed from this pulpit, as though we were anxious about you, may be relieved for once not to be in the center of attention. Childhood and youth do have their problems, but today I am talking to my own generation. We came out of good homes, let us say; we were not ill-treated in our childhood; were not wrecked by the temptations of adolescence; and now, so some would think, we have only to ride the smooth currents of maturity to the end.

That is a dangerous falsehood. The temptations of maturity are as real and as ruinous as the temptations of youth. More obituaries than one likes to think, if they were honest, would say: "This man began to build, and was not able to finish." A good beginning never implies a good ending, for the qualities which enable a man to start well are not the same qualities which enable him to carry on well to the end. A man can start on any enterprise if he is eager, ardent, hopeful, enthusiastic, susceptible to the thrill of new adventure; but, if the enterprise lasts a long time and faces difficulty, as all worth-while enterprises do, he must have other attributes if he is to come to a fine finish— constancy, patience, perseverance, courage, steadfastness. How many good starters there are in comparison with good finishers!

Family life illustrates this truth. What does it take to set the wedding bells ringing and to begin a family? Youth, passion, romance, ardor—any day they will launch a family with flags flying and friends cheering. What does it take to see a family through to a fine end? Fidelity, constancy, mutual forbearance, love deepening into friendship strong as steel and beautiful as music. Alas for those families concerning which the old word is true: This home began to build, but was not able to finish!

Any person who comes through to his maturity has to face, one way or another, this range of facts which we are considering. We may well talk honestly with our own souls about it.

For one thing, many of us in our maturity face the temptation of misused power. In our youth we did not have it to misuse. We often wondered what we would succeed in doing with our lives. We had premonitory hours filled with vague imaginings about the future, but how could we tell? Once Napoleon Bonaparte played with the idea of being a bookseller. That is a picture for the imagination to work upon—Napoleon Bonaparte selling books—and yet how true an illustration it is of the baffling uncertainty of every youth, wondering what latent powers are in his life to be elicited and used!

Some of us when we were young determined to find out. We did not throw away our early years. We began to build. I am well enough acquainted with the life story of some of you to know that, in consequence, far beyond anything you dreamed, power has come into your hands, in your profession, your business, or in public life. You are Bonaparte at least thus far, that emerging from a humble home in some Corsica, you thought you might do this small thing or that, and now see what unexpected and wide influence is in your hand! And just at that point, Bonaparte went to pieces, not in his youth, but in his maturity, mishandling power.

Some lives are as we love to picture them—streams that flow out from an early turbulence of rapid and cascade into the calm waters of maturity. But some lives are like the Niagara, beginning with a deep, still current full of quiet power, and in its latter course breaking into such rapids and waterfalls as no young stream could ever know; or like the Mississippi, that begins in multitudinous peaceful rivulets and ends with a capacity for ruinous floods which governments of states and nation hardly can control. The most difficult temptations in human life are not adolescent. They are inherent in the power that comes into some men's hands in maturity.

Again, some of us in our maturity face the temptation to lose our idealism and religious faith. Youth's trouble with religion is very real, but youth has qualities which suggest and encourage some kind of spiritual faith. For healthy youth is naturally eager, enthusiastic, hopeful, idealistic. Its difficulties with faith in God are commonly intellectual, but not cynical and disillusioned, and so healthy youth forever tends to escape from religion into religion and, throwing over old forms of church and faith, to find still that without faith one cannot keep genuinely young.

Said a leading Harvard student, "Dreiser, Mencken, Sinclair Lewis, Hemingway and the others of that school we have put aside as too destructive. We want to build up. Among my associates, the literary group, I haven't met a student who is an atheist. They all believe in God, but the problem is the approach to God. We don't find it in the existing churches, and we want it. If some man would show us the way, we'd run to him." To be sure! Irreligion, atheism, materialism, cynicism stand in direct contradiction to the natural hopefulness, eagerness and idealism of youth. After every spiritual slump you can count on youth's coming back one way or another to some kind of idealistic faith.

If someone says, however, that this hopeful thing, being true, solves our problem, I protest that it is a fairy tale to think that because a man keeps his faith through the intellectual difficulties of his youth and brings it out into his maturity, he is going to live happily with it ever after. The great collapses of faith are not in youth; they are in maturity, and some of you here this morning understand why.

Maturity knows about life so much more terrific and tragic things than youth can ever know. A fortunate youth is like a newly launched ship, still bedecked with the flags and bunting of its gay beginning, but age is an old ship that has seen furious storms, its joints strained by the sea's pounding, and its memories sobered by many a foundered wreck. One of our distinguished modern atheists, Dreiser, has told us of the fine idealism with which he began in youth, and then says, "Up to this time there had been in me a blazing and unchecked desire to get on and the feeling that in doing so we did get somewhere; now in its place was the definite conviction that spiritually we got nowhere, that there was no hereafter, that one lived and had his being because one had to, and that it was of no importance." That man began to build but he was not able to finish.

When we are through, then, talking about, sympathizing with and worrying over the spiritual struggles of adolescence, remember that any man who faces the difficulties, tragedies, bereavements which inevitably come in maturity has to pass through a second spiritual adolescence. No man, if he is to live well, can escape this. It is faith enlarging its grasp and deepening its meaning to take in the more tremendous facts with which maturity presents us. It is a man getting his second wind in the long race of life. It is a ship going out through the smooth waters of the inner bay to the long rollers and sometimes the howling storms of the Atlantic. It is the spirit having to decide, when the wind rises, whether it will blow out his fire of faith or fan it to a greater conflagration.

When I think what some of you are facing—the anxieties that beset you, the bereavements that have broken up your homes, the tragedies that have befallen you or those whom you most dearly love—I know that in your youth you never had such a struggle to keep your faith. Your childhood was like a sheltered valley but now the road winds up to dangerous altitudes and on bleak and windy crests tempests at times blow, the like of which you never dreamed in youth. You know now why the New Testament says, "He that endures to the end will be saved."

This is an inescapable issue in every great life. Jesus did not escape it. He began amid the flowers of Galilee where it was not difficult to hold an idealistic faith, but before he was through he had to be able on a cross to say, "It is finished." Long ago you and I began to build a sustaining Christian faith. What will be said of us at last—"He was not able to finish"?

Again, some of us in our maturity face the temptation to self-complacency, cocksureness, spiritual pride. Of course youth is dangerous, but, then, youth knows it. The temptations of youth advertise themselves as such. Stormy and passionate, only a fool can mistake their peril. Moreover, an aspiring youth understands that he has not yet made his way in the world and that it will require all the grace and grit, the character and reputation he can achieve. Alert and resolute, the best of youth go out to win their spurs. But we have completed that struggle. We are established now in a habit of life that personally brings us peace, professionally brings us recognition, financially brings us security. We have successfully negotiated the dangerous moral rapids of adolescence and now are safe out, we think, in the smooth waters of maturity. Safe! At precisely that point multitudes go to pieces.

Self-complacency starts it. When a writer has made a resounding success with his first book, is his problem ended? It has only just begun. A friend once said to William Dean Howells about a writer who had made an extraordinary initial success, "His laurels are faded." "Yes," said Howells, "he has been resting on them." So resting on our laurels, we grow happily satisfied with ourselves. Then we relax our care about the old safeguards, the faiths, fellowships, spiritual practices that once we counted on to keep our character. When we were young we had a practical use for our Christianity because sometimes passionate temptations came up against our souls like an army with banners. We felt like beleaguered soldiers who have fired their last round of ammunition and fear that, if the foe comes again, they will give in. But now, feeling secure and safe in our acquired success, we question what there is to fear. So we relax our guard. Happily satisfied about ourselves, relaxing our guard—then what? Then we increase the moral strain. There is serious truth in that phrase about the "dangerous forties." Yes, if you keep your eyes open, you can extend it into the dangerous fifties. There were practices when we were young that we did not fool with because we did not dare, but now we have come safely on, we are respected by our friends—what have we to fear? So we increase the moral strain. Happily satisfied about ourselves, relaxing our guard, increasing the strain—then what? Then someday there is a crash and we go to pieces.

It would be astonishing if here this morning some such catastrophe were not in course of preparation. Only this last week I struggled, as it were, with blood and tears to prevent a friend from such imminent disaster. Someone here is likely to recapitulate the agelong story of Hannibal, who conquered the Alps but was overthrown by Capua.

My friend, you made a fairly clean hit in youth, did you not? You got to first base, ran to second; today you are on third; and you are going to be caught napping off third when all your friends are expecting you to get home.

Misused power, lost faith, foolish complacency—these are some of the temptations of maturity. Who, however, in such a time

as ours, could talk on this theme and not think of another matter, discouragement about the world? If someone says that youth
also looks with sinking heart upon this disheveled, chaotic era,
I say, Yes, but youth rarely suffers from a sinking heart long at
a time. Youth is resilient. It has resources of energy to fall back
upon. It is as naturally hopeful as sunrise or springtime. But in
maturity to fall upon a time like this! One of the saddest tragedies
of this chaotic, violent, atomic age is not often talked about, but
it is real: many people, namely, who would otherwise have
grown old beautifully, who are going out into their autumn days
saddened, hopeless, discouraged about the world. They are not
going to finish well. Cicero's great work on old age, *De Senec-
tute,* is a classic, yet even Cicero did not escape this temptation
of elder years. He died when he was only sixty-three, but even
before that he had written, "Old age makes me more and more
bitter." Some of us, too, are not going to finish well.

Such an ending is a pity after a good start. A visitor in India
was entertained by an Indian lady of high rank. The visitor was
so impressed with her charm and grace that she could not for-
bear saying, "I think you are perfectly beautiful," to which the
Indian lady quietly replied, "I ought to be beautiful, my dear.
I am seventy-four years old." What a philosophy—I ought to be
beautiful; I am seventy-four years old!

Make no mistake about it: the grandeur of a great life lies
in a fine finish.

We are celebrating Washington's birthday this week—a man
who began to build and was able to finish. He went through
desperate days, as when Arnold betrayed the cause or despair
stalked the camp at Valley Forge, that might well have broken
down his nerve. He won victories so unexpected and resplendent
and rose to heights so dangerous to moral poise that he might

well have had his head turned, if it had not been as steady as
the mountain that now bears his name. He faced as bitter personal hatred and vituperation as any president of the United
States has ever faced, and through it all he kept his dignity. He
came at last to a place whose power a little man would have
misused to selfish ends or clung to to please his vanity but,
gladly relinquishing which, he left behind him one of the outstanding records of unselfishness in history. He had staying
power. He was calm when others were excited, hopeful when
others were discouraged, determined when others were growing
weak. To be sure, he had a fine start. At the age of twenty-one
was he not appointed Adjutant-General for the Southern District
of Virginia? But that is not half the story. He was able to finish.

For years now we have been worrying about the younger
generation. Let us today tackle the problem of ourselves! The
younger generation seems to me very promising, and they would
certainly find it easier to be better, if we, the mature, stood up
to the situation that confronts us as we ought to stand, un-
spoiled, undisillusioned, undiscouraged. Shakespeare was right:

> Let me not live,
> After my flame lacks oil, to be the snuff
> Of younger spirits.

When Dias discovered the southern point of Africa, he encountered such tempests that he named the promontory the
Cape of Storms. But the vast importance of having a sea route
to India was soon recognized and that name was changed from
Cape of Storms to Cape of Good Hope. If we were half the men
our fathers were, if we could rise a little into the creative faith
with which they met and overcame the tempests of their day,
if we could have in this nation now a revival of constructive,

sacrificial citizenship, we might find that we too have been rounding the Cape of Good Hope.

Meanwhile, one of the strongest arguments for Christianity is a Christian who thus comes beautifully to the end, able to finish, demonstrating that,

> E'en to old age all my people shall prove
> My sovereign, eternal, unchangeable love.

Faith and Immortality

CHRISTIAN belief in immortality is a corollary of the total Christian faith. It is not the initial affirmation of the Christian creed, nor is it a detachable item that can be held in isolation; it is an involved consequence, part and parcel of the whole Christian view of life. Uniformly the great creeds begin in substance like this: I believe in God; I believe in Jesus Christ; I believe in the Holy Spirit; I believe in the communion of saints; and then, after such affirmations, they add, I believe in the life everlasting. That logically follows. If one holds the Christian philosophy of life as a whole, one cannot finish with purposeless transiency as the last word and with no prospect for the soul except a dead-end street.

Of course immortality can be believed in without this context of Christian faith. Probably the first belief in life after death emerged among primitive men who in their dreams saw and heard the dead, whom they had known, acting and speaking still; and like all primitives, accepting dream-life as authentic, they were convinced that the dead were not dead. In many diverse contexts faith in immortality of one kind or another has arisen, but it was not Christian faith. That is a corollary of the total Christian view of life.

This fact that the Christian idea of life everlasting is a member of a family of ideas, a genetically related household of con-

victions, explains why many cannot believe it. That Christian
family of ideas is not in their heads; they hold a contrasting
philosophy or have only a vague vacuum where a philosophy of
life ought to be; they do not and cannot hold the *Christian* faith
in life everlasting; and yet they inevitably face the fact of death.
What about death? "If a man die, shall he live again?" That
question they confront, whatever family of ideas they have in
their heads.

Many people today answer that question not so much with
convictions, not so much with a total philosophy of life, as with
moods. Who has not noted these moods in his friends? Who
has not experienced them himself?

Some feel that we would do well to satisfy ourselves with one
life, make what we can of that, and not be concerned with any
other. When Henry D. Thoreau was on his deathbed, his friend
Parker Pillsbury asked him whether he could see anything on
the other side. "One world at a time, Parker," said Thoreau,
"one world at a time." That mood is familiar.

Others feel no desire for life after death. Life here has been
so difficult for them that, when they are through, they want to
be through. So Swinburne put it:

> From too much love of living,
>   From hope and fear set free,
> We thank with brief thanksgiving
>   Whatever gods may be
> That no life lives forever;
> That dead men rise up never;
> That even the weariest river
>   Winds somewhere safe to sea.

That mood is not commonly shouted aloud, but it is familiar.

Others feel that they have never seen pictured any future world which they would be particularly interested to inhabit—certainly not the traditionally portrayed heaven of pearly gates, golden streets and endless singing. They are in revolt against the glib, superficial certainty which some people, possessing no more bona fide information than anybody else, describe what Reinhold Niebuhr called "the furniture of heaven and the temperature of hell"; describe with dogmatic exactitude the conditions of the future life—"clergymen's heavens," as one man put it, "which members of other professions might find something of a strain." That mood is not uncommon.

Others resent the self-centeredness involved in looking forward to a future world to reward them for being good. They recall Seneca, the Stoic, who in one of his parables tells of a mariner, wrestling with a storm-tossed boat, and saying, "O Neptune, Thou canst save me if Thou wilt, or Thou canst drown me; but whether or no, I will hold my rudder true." Is not that, some feel, a nobler motive than working for a heavenly crown? We will do right because it is right, they say; we will hold our rudder true whatever comes; and you may keep your dreams of a future paradise to pay you for your goodness, if you need that incentive. That mood is not uncommon.

Others feel that faith in immortality encourages otherworldliness, whereas this world with its opportunities and tasks should engage our whole attention. They used to hear that, without faith in immortality, they would plunge into self-indulgence, would eat, drink and be merry, for tomorrow they die, but they do not think that true. Let us work for mankind, they say, and as for the future think not of any immortality of our own personalities—which Einstein called "ridiculously egotistical"—but think of immortality of influence, a blessed heritage of good work done to be handed on to our children after us. In one of our major colleges a professor said to his classes: "The modern belief in immortality costs more than it is worth . . . its disappearance from among the most civilized nations would be, on the whole, a gain." That mood, especially in certain academic circles, is familiar.

What is the trouble which the Christian finds in these negative moods? There is a measure of truth in every one of them, and yet there is something deeply the matter with them. They lack a world view, so the Christian is convinced. They lack a total philosophy of life. They are moods—natural moods, which we all understand—but they have not grappled with the problem of life's ultimate meaning. They are sidestepping the profoundest questions which the human mind must ask about the nature of reality. They belong either to no family of ideas or to the wrong family of ideas about this universe.

Let me, for a moment, be autobiographical. In my boyhood the idea of immortality, the thought that I must go on living forever, was to me appalling. In imagination I pictured with terror that endless necessity of living with myself—no death final, no suicide conclusive, no way out of going on and on and on everlastingly, no escape from that eternal waking up again to find myself living with myself. I was, in effect, a Buddhist, counting the endless recurrence of rebirths the supreme horror from which there must be some way to escape. Even yet when I hear someone talking about immortality as though it meant merely John Smith going on living with John Smith forever and forever, I cry out for some Nirvana as a hopeful alternative. So George Bernard Shaw, in his *Back to Methuselah*, makes Adam say:

If only I can be relieved of having to endure myself forever! If only the care of this terrible garden may pass on to some other gardener. . . . If only the rest and sleep that enable me to bear it from day to day, could grow after many days into an eternal rest, an eternal sleep, then I could face my days, however long they may last. Only there must be some end, some end! I am not strong enough to bear eternity.

I wonder if anybody believes in immortality intelligently and seriously who has not gone through that stage.

If now I do believe in immortality it is because of two considerations: first, that life eternal in the context of the Christian faith has dimensions and meanings utterly beyond our power to imagine, so that those adolescent, Buddhistic fears of mine were nonsense; and second, that immortality is not merely an affirmation about me and my survival of death, but about the total meaning of this universe. I believe in immortality now, not because of any obsessive craving for it for myself, but because it belongs to the only family of ideas that makes sense out of life as a whole.

Without immortality all the best we know on earth will in the end be utterly lost. Faith in immortality, some say, is merely an opiate, a psychological shot-in-the-arm, a wishful solace for our private grief. No! Far from being merely that, faith in immortality faces, as most philosophies pretending to be realistic never face, the most drastic and momentous fact about this planet, as well as every other planet. It is temporary. That is the ultimate fact about this planet—it is temporary. Once uninhabitable, it will sometime be uninhabitable again. What Shakespeare put into sonorous lines is now confirmed by science:

> The cloud-capp'd towers, the gorgeous palaces,
> The solemn temples, the great globe itself,

> Yea, all which it inherit, shall dissolve
> And, like this insubstantial pageant faded,
> Leave not a rack behind. . . .

Scientists used to say that would happen because the sun's heat, slowly dissipated, would end at last and the earth freeze up. Now they are saying that the sun before it cools will first grow hotter and hotter, so that the earth will burn up. But whatever the method, the fact is clear—there will not always be even the planet, earth.

In the end, therefore, if the best is not to be lost, there is only one way out. If this earth is, as Keats said, a "vale of Soul-making," and if the souls that grow to character and strength and beauty here are not annihilated by death; if, like a schoolhouse, this earth perishes but those who are trained in it go on; then and only then the best in the end will not be lost.

None of the substitutes for personal immortality meet this situation. The immortality of memory—that is beautiful, the cherished recollection of "all the saints who from their labors rest"; the immortality of influence—that is splendid in those blessed dead who "live again in lives made better by their presence"; but on a transient earth, no memory and no influence are immortal; they are transient too. Unless the best in creation, as we know it, is to end in annihilation and futility, immortality must be true.

Consider, first, that this faith in immortality meets a profound intellectual need. To say that in the end the best is doomed to be lost, does something, not simply to our hearts but to our minds. The central motive of the intellectual life is to find the meaning of things. Concerning the simplest physical fact, studied in a laboratory, the scientific mind feels sure that it has a meaning if we could but discover it. And from such single items in the universe, to the whole cosmos itself man's mind moves out, driven by an inner conviction that there must be meaning there. Not a preacher but a scientist, describing the attitudes of his fellow scientists, said this: "They would like to feel that this enterprise of life upon which we have embarked without any volition on our part, is a worth-while process. They would like to think of it as something more than an endless procession of life out of and into the dark." That desire for meaning is a hunger not simply of the heart, but of the mind. As William James of Harvard said: "This life . . . *feels* like a real fight . . . in which something is eternally gained for the universe by success."

Unless immortality is true, however, nothing can be eternally gained, but everything we value most will stop in a blind alley, a dead-end street. Then all our forefathers ended in a blind alley; and all whom we have loved long since and lost awhile—they ended in a blind alley; and we ourselves, and our children and children's children, and at last the whole earth will end in a dead-end street—no thoroughfare, nothing coming out of it, no ultimate meaning.

That this amazing cosmos should be as irrational, senseless and futile as that, I cannot make myself believe. A professor at one of our prominent American universities said once that all the personalities earth has known or will know are only like snowflakes falling on a river. So! Snowflakes falling on a river! The river, of course, is the endless sweep of materialistic energy, and all that is precious and memorable on earth—the great minds, the great characters—are only snowflakes falling on it, and that too is the final summation and significance of Christ himself, a snowflake on a river! That does something not simply to our emotions but to our minds. So one of the most lovable of men, Somerset Maugham, who has entertained us all with his stories, accepting this philosophy, sums up thus his final creed: "There is no reason for life and life has no meaning."

Think of going out to face these tremendous days with such a slogan on our banners: "There is no reason for life and life has no meaning." It will not do! The facts that we call spiritual —goodness, truth, beauty, the marvel of great minds, the splendor of great character—are just as real as the facts we call physical, and in one case as in the other there must be an adequate explanation. That is the basic conviction of our intellectual life: that for everything there must be an adequate explanation. And to dismiss Christ and all that he represents in human life as a snowflake on a river is not adequate—not emotionally adequate, but not intellectually adequate either. It takes more than that to account for him. The best in this universe is the revelation of the deepest in it, and the universe will not throw it away —that alone puts sense and meaning into life. Faith in immortality is more than solace for private grief. As John Fiske of Harvard said, it is the "supreme act of faith in the reasonableness of God's work."

This leads us to note, in the second place, that faith in immortality meets not only in general a profound intellectual but in particular a profound theological need. Whatever special name we may give to the Power, not ourselves, behind and in this universe, that Power is real; and here this morning we may take it for granted that we are theists, calling that Power "God." Consider, then, what a momentous difference belief or disbelief in immortality makes to our concept of God!

Some people suppose that faith in immortality is egotistical. A man, they say, must be absurdly obsessed with his own importance to think he ought to live forever. That, however, is an utterly mistaken focusing of the matter. What denial of immortality does to me is nothing compared with what it does to God. It makes him a God of unfinished business. On a planet where, as one scientist put it, "nothing will remain, not even the ruins," to deny immortality makes the Creator a God of the fugitive and transitory only—the whole story of this planet in the end unfinished business. He creates a world full of possibilities —promising, prophetic possibilities—great personality, open doors to truth and goodness, vistas with no horizons visible. These possibilities are here; they have arrived but, without immortality, they do not survive. In the end nothing comes of them. They have no completion, no consummation. God begins everything and finishes nothing. What kind of God is that?

Schubert, dying at thirty-one and leaving his *Unfinished Symphony*, is a parable of human life. Even if you don't die at thirty-one, but live to be as old as the Psalmist's span, still there is an unfinished symphony. Corot, the artist, when he was seventy-seven years old, said: "If the Lord lets me live two years longer I think I can paint something beautiful." Here, indeed, is the deep mystery of human life—that while our bodies are the natural prey of death, our minds and spirits already have started on a road that has no visible terminus. The more truth we learn, the more truth we see to learn. The more goodness we achieve, the more goodness we see there is to achieve. Such realms are essentially eternal. Death has no relevance to them. The farther we go in them, the farther there is to go. William James of Harvard said once that his interest in personal immortality was not of the keenest order, but that as he grew older his belief in it grew stronger, and when asked why, he answered, "Because I am just getting fit to live."

This basic fact about life plainly involves God. We Americans blame ourselves because we waste the resources of our continent, but if death ends all, then of all wasters God is the worst. He forever produces spirits and throws them away half finished. He creates capacities he never uses, possibilities he never fulfills. He makes the most valuable thing we know—personality—and leaves it unfinished business. He launches ships he does not sail; he blows soap bubbles and watches them burst. I don't believe it. I know all the difficulties that confront faith in immortality. It is a great mystery. I do not think that any picture we have of it can possibly be true. We are like unborn babes in a mother's womb. What faces them is not death but birth; yet it is birth into a world not a single detail of which could they possibly imagine. What eye hath not seen, what ear hath not heard, and what hath not entered into the heart of man, that has God prepared—Paul is right about that. But Paul is right about another thing: "This mortal must put on immortality." God is not the God of unfinished business.

In India, they tell us, there are fakirs who sit beside pools of water with piles of colored dust beside them and so skillfully drop the dust upon the still surface that they make for you recognizable portraits of distinguished characters. Then the breeze ruffles the pool and the picture disappears. Is that God's business? Does he take colored dust and drop it on life's water and, lo! Plato, or Isaiah, or Christ himself, or nearer souls whom we have known and loved! and then does the breeze disturb the water and they disappear? That would be a strange business for God!

Without faith in immortality, a closed door is the ultimate symbol of this universe—a closed door for every individual life, a closed door for every generation's life, a closed door at last for all life. The ultimate symbol of this vast creative process, of which we are a part, a closed door! I don't believe it. Certainly faith in the Christian God makes that impossible. He is essentially the God of open doors, with "the eternal purpose which he purposed in Christ."

So far we have been saying that faith in immortality is no mere egotistical greediness to go on living, no mere private solace in time of grief, but is of profound concern to our whole philosophy of life and our whole concept of God. Now let us go on to say that it is of profound concern also to our social life and all our democratic hopes and values.

During World War II I conversed with an American journalist who had covered the news in Berlin up to our very entrance into the war. Here in essence is what that journalist said to me: I came home from Berlin and went back to my old college campus, and I said to some of the professors there, You are teaching these students here the philosophy that has made Nazi Germany what she is. You tried to teach me that only a few years ago—a godless materialism that makes the physical the source and end of everything, that undermines the bases of moral principle and makes of the whole universe a purposeless machine. And now in Nazidom I have seen what happens when that philosophy really gets going and comes to its logical conclusion, and I have come back to tell you that the stuff you are teaching here is about the most dangerous dynamite that is being scattered around the world.

That journalist, in my judgment, is right in seeing that the materialistic philosophy with its denial of God and immortality does change the whole climate of man's thought and life, so that democracy, for example, which rests upon a deep conviction concerning human value, dignity and possibility, loses the very soil it must have to grow in.

I do not mean that were faith in immortality to vanish altogether from the earth we would not go on living for good causes here. Of course we would. The best of us would resign ourselves to the ultimate meaninglessness of life as a whole and, so far as we could, forgetting that, we would try to make this earth while it lasted—and that will be for a long while—as livable a place as possible. But without faith in anything eternally worth while, what a change would take place in the moral and spiritual climate!

If someone says, But there are good men and women now, not believing in immortality, who are admirable public servants, I answer, Surely, there are. But they are unwittingly sustained by the faith of millions who still are sure that life is ultimately worth while, not merely a procession out of and into the dark. The faith that in the end the best will not be lost is in the very air we breathe. Our heritage is full of it; our great heroes have believed it; our literature enshrines it; its voice resounds around the earth on Easter Day; its quiet reassurance supports the minds and hearts of multitudes; and it has created a climate in which some great things have grown. The idea that every personality is sacred has grown in that climate—and democracy's belief in the value of individual people, so that our test of any social order is what it does to persons, one by one. The best in our Western democracy has come from two main sources—the great Greeks, with their profound faith in the soul and its eternal meaning; and the Jewish-Christian tradition, with its central conviction that things seen are temporal, the things unseen, eternal. Immortality is the supreme assertion of the worth of personality; and that faith has created a climate in which the very liberties and democracies we fight for now have grown.

More things are wrought by climate than we stop to think. Bishop McConnell says that as a boy he was fascinated by a book in his father's library, filled with pictures of old dinosaurs and monstrous reptiles that once roamed the earth; and that he used to wonder how ever they were got rid of in the end. Then, when he went to college, he found out: the climate changed; that was what happened, a change in climate, so that the old beasts died off.

Well, faith in immortality affects tremendously the spiritual climate. Picture a world where everybody is convinced that all the noblest souls that are the glory of our race are only snowflakes falling on a river. Picture a world where everybody holds Somerset Maugham's creed, that in the long run "there is no reason for life and life has no meaning." Picture our race unanimously convinced that every personality and at last every social gain ends in a blind alley; that, as one honest atheist says, man "has no reason to suppose that his own life has any more meaning than the life of the humblest insect that crawls from one annihilation to another." The major effect of that would be to change the whole climate of human life.

To me the most dreadful thing about materialism is its necessary declaration that the best elements in us, our finest qualities, are misfits in this universe, strange temporary accidents that do not belong here and do not correspond with the real facts. A professor at one of our prominent American universities, one of the most honest atheists of our time, puts it frankly: "It grows more and more likely that man must remain an ethical animal in a universe which contains no ethical element." Get that picture! It is the inevitable corollary of the materialistic philosophy—man an ethical animal in a universe that contains no ethical element. Yes, man an intellectual animal in a universe that contains no intellectual element; man a purposeful animal in a universe that contains no purposeful element; man a loving animal in a universe that contains not the slightest shred of goodwill; all our best ethical life a chance intruder, a transient misfit, as Bertrand Russell calls it, "a curious accident in a backwater"—that is the materialistic creed and it creates a climate in which the best social hopes of mankind will only with desperate difficulty manage to survive.

Listen to Beatrice Webb about this. She and her husband some fifteen years ago wrote one of the most understanding books about communism in the English language. She is a highly intelligent liberal. Listen to her then, all the more, on this subject: "I cannot help having a half-conscious conviction that, if the human race is mortal, if its existence is without aim, if that existence is to end, at however remote a period, in a complete dissolution, like that which overcomes the individual, then life indeed is not worth living—not worth living to the mass of mankind."

That is the climate which materialism produces. Over against *that*, here is a philosophy which supports man's best—that spiritual life does belong in this universe; that it is a revelation of what eternally is so; that Christ and all he stands for are no accidental interlopers on this scene; that he came from the eternal, reveals the eternal, and lives still in the eternal; that as Emerson cried,

> . . . what is excellent,
> As God lives, is permanent!

That philosophy creates a climate in which mankind's best social hopes can grow.

In conclusion, however, we must of course recognize the fact that faith in immortality is relevant not only to profound intellectual, theological and social problems, but to profound personal needs as well. That is where most people begin to face the issue. Edna St. Vincent Millay speaks for all of us when she says:

> I am not resigned to the shutting away of loving
>   hearts in the hard ground.
> So it is, and so it will be, for so it has been,
>   time out of mind:
> Into the darkness they go, the wise and the
>   lovely. Crowned
> With lilies and with laurel they go; but I am not
>   resigned.
>
> .   .   .   .
>
> Down, down, down into the darkness of the grave
> Gently they go, the beautiful, the tender, the kind;
> Quietly they go, the intelligent, the witty, the brave.
> I know. But I do not approve. And I am not resigned.[1]

There speaks the human soul in its deepest hours.

Note, however, that even that personal cry for life eternal is not primarily egotistical. It is the cry not of egotism but of love, caring so much for someone else that death must not be the end of such a life.

Professor George Herbert Palmer of Harvard was a great teacher of philosophy; he believed in immortality, knew all the

---

[1] "Dirge without Music" from *The Buck in the Snow and Other Poems* by Edna St. Vincent Millay. Copyright, 1928, by Edna St. Vincent Millay. Published by Harper & Brothers. Used by permission of Brandt & Brandt.

arguments pro and con and could present them with clarity and force. But I suspect that the real source of his faith in life eternal was best revealed, not in any lecture on philosophy he ever gave, but in something he said when his wife died: Who would "not call the world irrational if out of deference to a few particles of disordered matter it excludes so fair a spirit?" Not egotism but love speaks here its inevitable word, sure that in God's world things unseen, beautiful beyond our power to tell, and of value infinite, must be eternal.

Plato's *Phaedo* is the greatest argument for immortality in the ancient world, but Plato and his friends were thinking, not first about themselves, but about Socrates whom they loved. Death ought not to be the end of him. The New Testament is radiant with eternal hope, but those first disciples, far from thinking about themselves, were saying about Christ that death had no dominion over him. Always when faith in immortality rises strong and confident, its source is not egotism but love—Tennyson writing *In Memoriam,*

> Thou madest man, he knows not why,
> He thinks he was not made to die;
> And thou hast made him: thou art just,

because Tennyson cared so much for Arthur Hallam; Ralph Waldo Emerson writing in his *Threnody* the words I just quoted,

> . . . what is excellent,
> As God lives, is permanent!

because he cared so deeply for his little son whom death had taken.

In the last analysis our belief in immortality springs from our love of people. And love is *not* blind; it has eyes to see in loved ones prophecies that ought to be fulfilled, fine things growing that should not be lost in an eternal winter with no springtime.

So we come back to our first affirmation that faith in immortality is not an isolated, detachable item in the Christian creed but a member of a great family of ideas: a meaningful universe, a purposeful God, a world where man's social hopes will not end in utter annihilation, and so personality sacred, with endless possibilities.

People say that we cannot imagine or picture immortality. They are right. Waste no time on charlatans who think they can! People say that we cannot demonstrate immortality. They are right. Demonstration, strictly speaking, involves verification, and in the nature of the case that is impossible now. Neither immortality nor its opposite can in a scientific sense be proved. People say, Let us live to the full now and not worry too much about immortality. So say I. Goethe, who hoped so deeply for immortality that he said once, "Those are dead even for this life who hope for no other," said to his friend, Eckermann: "An able man, who has something regular to do here, and must toil and struggle and produce day by day, leaves the future world to itself, and is active and useful in this." So say I.

But underneath and overhead and through this present life, like sunshine which one does not always think of but which is here, runs a strong conviction that vivifies and illumines and dignifies everything, that spiritual life is eternal and that ahead of it the doors are open. That is all we need to know, that ahead the doors are open. Sure of that, "I do not ask to see the future scene; one step enough for me."

If you want it summed up in homely words, recall Thornton Wilder's expression of his faith, in his play *Our Town*:

I don't care what they say with their mouths—everybody knows that *something* is eternal. And it ain't houses and it ain't names, and it ain't earth, and it ain't even stars—everybody knows in their bones that *something* is eternal, and *that* something has to do with human beings. All the greatest people ever lived have been telling us that for five thousand years and yet you'd be surprised how people are always losing hold of it. There's something way down deep that's eternal about every human being.

Set in Linotype Fairfield
Format by Robert Cheney
Manufactured by The Haddon Craftsmen, Inc.
Published by HARPER & BROTHERS, New York